Air Fryer Cookbook for Beginners

Delicious, Quick & Easy Recipes to Save Time, Eat Healthy, and Enjoy Cooking

Air Fryer Cookbook for Beginners

PUBLISHED BY: Mark Evans
Copyright © 2019 All rights reserved.

No part of this publication may be copied, reproduced in any format, by any means, electronic or otherwise, without prior consent from the copyright owner and publisher of this book.

Table of Contents

Introduction 4

Chapter 1: Air Fryer 5

Chapter 2: Breakfast Recipes 10

Chapter 3: Lunch Recipes 30

Chapter 4: Side Dish Recipes 49

Chapter 5: Snack and Appetizer Recipes 67

Chapter 6: Fish and Seafood Recipes 86

Chapter 7: Poultry Recipes 106

Chapter 8: Meat Recipes 125

Chapter 9: Vegetable Recipes 149

Chapter 10: Dessert Recipes 163

Conclusion 181

Thank you 182

Introduction

This cookbook is the ultimate companion book to any air fryer. Inside, you will find a wonderful selection of traditional, modern, and alternative recipes. This air fryer cookbook is devoted to both beginner cooks and advanced users. If you are looking for a proper guide for every kind of food you can cook in the air fryer, you should have this cookbook in your collection. With this air fryer cookbook, become an air fryer master and impress your family, friends and guests. This cookbook is comprised of a delicious collection of recipes that are suitable for all tastes. Each recipe is simple to make, very easy to cook, full of flavor, and offers a healthier alternative to traditionally fried foods.

Throughout the pages of this book, you will discover a variety of sweet, savory, salty, citrusy, and other delicious recipes. Weekend brunch, date night, or dinner with a friend – whatever the occasion, these tasty recipes are made to be shared together. Crispy on the outside, juicy on the inside, and easy to prep and cook – this air fryer cookbook combines everything you love about air frying with the easiest, everyday recipes to enjoy conveniently crispy and healthy meals. You are guaranteed to find a wonderful selection of traditional, modern, and mouthwatering recipes to suit any palate. So flip over to the next page and start making your own delicious, quick and easy meals that are healthy and better for you!

Chapter 1: Air Fryer

The air fryer was developed in 2008 in England. It is a stand-alone appliance that fries, bakes, cooks, grills and steams food to tender perfection. It consists of a heating element, a fan that pushes hot air around the food, and a frying basket. The heating element browns and crisps the exterior while cooking the interior to a safe final temperature.

The benefits of air frying:
1. Air frying is better for your health: The air fryer uses less oil to fry foods. You can use only a small amount of oil and achieve beautifully crisp results for chicken, fish, French fries, and more.

2. Hassel-free cooking: Thanks to its well-regulated temperature and automatic shutoff system, air frying requires virtually no monitoring. You only have to toss or flip food occasionally, and the device does all the work.
3. Minimal mess: The food basket is enclosed in the air fryer, so you don't have to use several pans or pots. Also, the air fryer basket is easy to clean.
4. Conveniently efficient: Air fryer cooking is ideal for busy nights. You don't need time-consuming appliances such as an oven or stove.
5. Time-saver: The air fryer is fast. It saves your valuable time. It is faster to cook using the air fryer than anything else.
6. Fast and easy cleaning: The cooking chamber and most of the air fryer components are dishwasher-safe.
7. More flavor: The flavor of fried food comes out in an air fryer. Food does not taste like the fat it is cooked in. You use only a small amount of oil, and the fried taste and texture is achieved.
8. Versatile cooking: The air fryer is more than just a fryer. You can grill, broil and bake in it too. Many users see the air fryer as a smaller convection oven than a fryer.
9. Safe: Air fryer is safe to use. Its components are food-safe, and the cooking process itself helps you avoid kitchen accidents that can result in injuries and burns.

Tips for usage:
1. Pat dry marinated foods before placing in the air fryer basket. This will help prevent smoke and splattering.
2. Don't overcrowd your air fryer. Give your food plenty of space so the air can circulate and cook your food properly.
3. Shake foods around. Shake foods during cooking, especially chips, French fries, and other smaller foods.
4. Spray foods with oil to prevent them from sticking to the air fryer basket.
5. Cook in batches if necessary.
6. You can preheat the device to allow it to heat up properly.
7. Lining the air fryer basket with parchment will minimize cleanup.
8. Use a baking pan for breaded foods.

Air-fryer safety:
- Read through the instruction manual for basic safety tips.
- Always place the air fryer on a stable, even and heat-proof surface.
- Keep your hands and face away from the vents.
- Never touch the basket or the pan it's attached to because they will be very hot.
- Never press the button holding the basket and pan together when you remove them.

Cleaning:
- The instruction manual will tell you how to clean and care for your machine.
- Let the machine cool down before attempting to clean.
- Remove the basket and pan and wash with soap, water, brush and a plastic scrubbing brush.
- Always check inside the appliance for bits of food and remove them.
- Wipe the appliance (turned off, unplugged and cooled down) both inside and outside with a damp towel, or paper towel.
- If oil has dripped to the bottom of the pan, soak it up with paper towels and then wipe clean.

Proper use, care and maintenance:
1. Read the manual. It is important that you read the manual.
2. Check the right power source/outlet. Otherwise, problems can happen.
3. Check the assembly of the appliance.
4. Follow the right procedures. Read the cooking instructions carefully and follow them.
5. Do not use harsh chemicals and cleaners on the air fryer.
6. Do not wash the air fryer immediately after use. Wait 30 minutes.

What if it's taking more time to cook?
The reasons are:
- Your pieces of meat or vegetables are larger than the recipe calls for.
- You are using a deeper cake pan than specified.
- You are doubling the recipe.

If the food is partly cooked:
- You need to cook food in one layer and in batches.

Chapter 2: Breakfast Recipes

Shrimp and Rice Breakfast Frittata

| Prep time: 15 minutes | Cook time: 15 minutes | Servings: 4 |

Ingredients

- Eggs – 4
- Pinch of salt
- Dried basil – ½ tsp.
- Cooked rice – ½ cup
- Chopped cooked shrimp – ½ cup
- Baby spinach – ½ cup
- Grated Monterey Jack cheese – ½ cup

Method

1. In a bowl, beat the eggs with salt and basil until frothy. Spray a 6x6x2-inch pan with nonstick cooking spray.
2. Combine the spinach, shrimp and rice in the prepared pan. Pour the eggs in and sprinkle with cheese.
3. Bake at 320F until frittata is puffed and golden brown, about 14 to 18 minutes.

Nutritional Facts Per Serving

- Calories: 226
- Fat: 9g
- Carb: 19g
- Protein: 16g

Omelette in Bread Cups

| Prep time: 12 minutes | Cook time: 11 minutes | Servings: 4 |

Ingredients

- Crusty rolls – 4 (3x4-inch)
- Gouda – 4 thin slices
- Eggs – 5
- Heavy cream – 2 tbsp.
- Dried thyme – ½ tsp.
- Precooked bacon – 3 strips, chopped
- Salt and ground pepper to taste

Method

1. Cut the tops off the rolls and remove the insides with your fingers to make a shell with about ½-inch of bread remaining. Line the rolls with a slice of cheese, pressing them gently, so the cheese conforms to the inside of the roll.

2. In a bowl, beat the eggs with the heavy cream until combined. Stir in the bacon, thyme, salt and pepper.
3. Spoon the egg mixture into the rolls over the cheese.
4. Bake at 330F until the eggs are puffy and starting to brown on top, about 8 to 12 minutes.

Nutritional Facts Per Serving

- Calories: 499
- Fat: 24g
- Carb: 46g
- Protein: 25g

Mixed Berry Muffins

Prep time: 15 minutes	Cook time: 15 minutes	Servings: 8

Ingredients

- Flour – 1 1/3 cups, plus 1 tbsp.
- Baking powder – 2 tsp.
- White sugar – ¼ cup
- Brown sugar – 2 tbsp.
- Eggs – 2
- Whole milk – 2/3 cup

- Safflower oil – 1/3 cup
- Mixed fresh berries – 1 cup

Method

1. Combine 1 1/3 cups flour, brown sugar, white sugar and baking powder in a bowl and mix well.
2. Combine the milk, eggs and oil in another bowl and beat until combined. Stir the egg mixture into the dry ingredients just until combined.
3. In another bowl, toss the mixed berries with the remaining 1 tbsp. flour until coated. Stir gently into the batter.
4. Double up 16 foil muffin cups to make 8 cups. Put 4 cups into the air fryer and fill ¾ full with the batter.
5. Bake at 320F until cooked, about 12 to 17 minutes.
6. Repeat with the remaining muffin cups and batter.
7. Cool and serve.

Nutritional Facts Per Serving

- Calories: 230
- Fat: 11g
- Carb: 30g
- Protein: 4g

Dutch Pancake

| Prep time: 12 minutes | Cook time: 15 minutes | Servings: 4 |

Ingredients

- Unsalted butter – 2 tbsp.
- Eggs – 3
- Flour – ½ cup
- Milk – ½ cup
- Vanilla – ½ tsp.
- Sliced fresh strawberries – 1 ½ cups
- Powdered sugar – 2 tbsp.

Method

1. Preheat the air fryer with a 6x6x2-inch pan in the basket. Add the butter and heat until the butter melts.
2. Meanwhile, beat the eggs, milk, flour and vanilla in a bowl until frothy.
3. Carefully remove the basket with the pan from the air fryer and tilt, so the butter covers the bottom of the pan. Pour in the batter and put back in the fryer.
4. Bake at 330F until the pancake is puffed and golden brown, about 12 to 16 minutes.
5. Remove and top with strawberries and powdered sugar.
6. Serve.

Nutritional Facts Per Serving

- Calories: 196
- Fat: 9g
- Carb: 22g
- Protein: 7g

Chocolate-Filled Doughnut Holes

Prep time: 10 minutes	Cook time: 12 minutes	Servings: 24

Ingredients

- Refrigerated biscuits – 1 (8-count) can
- Semisweet chocolate chips – 24 to 48
- Melted unsalted butter – 3 tbsp.
- Powdered sugar – ¼ cup

Method

1. Separate and cut each biscuit into thirds.
2. Flatten each biscuit piece slightly and put 1 to 2 chocolate chips in the center.
3. Wrap the dough around the chocolate and seal the edges well.
4. Brush each doughnut hole with a bit of butter.

5. Air-fry in batches at 340F for 8 to 12 minutes.
6. Remove and dust with powdered sugar.
7. Serve.

Nutritional Facts Per Serving

- Calories: 393
- Fat: 17g
- Carb: 55g
- Protein: 5g

Spinach and Cheese Omelette

Prep time: 5 minutes	Cook time: 8 minutes	Servings: 2

Ingredients

- Eggs – 3
- Shredded cheese – ½ cup
- Chopped fresh spinach – 2 tbsp.
- Salt and pepper to taste

Method

1. Whisk the eggs with salt and pepper and place in a flat oven-safe dish.

2. Add the cheese and spinach. Do not stir.
3. Cook at 390F for 8 minutes in the air fryer.
4. Check the consistency of the omelette. Cook for another 2 minutes if a browner omelette is desired.
5. Serve and enjoy.

Nutritional Facts Per Serving

- Calories: 209
- Fat: 15.9g
- Carb: 1g
- Protein: 15.4g

Quesadillas

| Prep time: 10 minutes | Cook time: 15 minutes | Servings: 4 |

Ingredients

- Eggs – 4
- Skim milk – 2 tbsp.
- Salt and pepper to taste
- Flour tortillas – 4
- Salsa – 4 tbsp.

- Cheddar cheese – 2 ounces, grated
- Small avocado – ½, peeled and thinly sliced

Method

1. Preheat the air fryer to 270F.
2. Beat together milk, eggs, salt and pepper.
3. Spray a 6x6-inch air fryer baking pan lightly with cooking spray and add egg mixture.
4. Cook for 8 to 9 minutes, stirring every 1 to 2 minutes, or until eggs are scrambled to your liking. Remove and set aside.
5. Spray one side of each tortilla with oil. Flip over.
6. Distribute cheese, salsa, eggs and avocado among the tortillas, covering only half of each tortilla.
7. Fold each tortilla in half and press down lightly.
8. Place 2 tortillas in air fryer basket and cook at 390F until cheese melts and outside feels slightly crispy, about 3 minutes. Repeat with the remaining two tortillas.
9. Cut each cooked tortilla into halves and serve.

Nutritional Facts Per Serving

- Calories: 231

- Fat: 14.7g
- Carb: 14.9g
- Protein: 11.5g

Tasty Baked Eggs

Prep time: 10 minutes	Cook time: 20 minutes	Servings: 4

Ingredients

- Eggs – 4
- Baby spinach – 1 pound, torn
- Ham – 7 ounces, chopped
- Milk – 4 tbsp.
- Olive oil – 1 tbsp.
- Cooking spray
- Salt and black pepper to taste

Method

1. Heat oil in a pan over medium heat. Add baby spinach and stir-fry for 2 minutes and remove from heat.
2. Grease 4 ramekins with cooking spray and distribute ham and baby spinach in each.
3. Crack an egg in each ramekin and add milk. Season with salt and pepper.

4. Place ramekins in the preheated air fryer at 350F and bake for 20 minutes.
5. Serve.

Nutritional Facts Per Serving

- Calories: 321
- Fat: 6g
- Carb: 15g
- Protein: 12g

Delicious Breakfast Soufflé

| Prep time: 10 minutes | Cook time: 8 minutes | Servings: 4 |

Ingredients

- Eggs – 4, whisked
- Heavy cream – 4 tbsp.
- Red chili pepper – 1 pinch, crushed
- Parsley – 2 tbsp., chopped
- Chives – 2 tbsp., chopped
- Salt and black pepper to taste

Method

1. In a bowl, mix eggs with chives, parsley, red chili pepper, heavy cream, salt and pepper. Mix well and divide into 4 soufflé dishes.
2. Arrange dishes in the air fryer and cook at 350F for 8 minutes.
3. Serve hot.

Nutritional Facts Per Serving

- Calories: 300
- Fat: 7g
- Carb: 15g
- Protein: 6g

Tasty Cinnamon Toast

| Prep time: 10 minutes | Cook time: 5 minutes | Servings: 6 |

Ingredients

- Butter – 1 stick, soft
- Bread – 12 slices
- Sugar – ½ cup
- Vanilla extract – 1 ½ tsp.

- o Cinnamon powder – 1 ½ tsp.

Method

1. In a bowl, mix soft butter with cinnamon, vanilla and sugar, and whisk well.
2. Spread this on bread slices, place them in the air fryer and cook at 400F for 5 minutes.
3. Serve.

Nutritional Facts Per Serving

- o Calories: 221
- o Fat: 4g
- o Carb: 12g
- o Protein: 8g

Turkey Burrito

Prep time: 10 minutes	Cook time: 10 minutes	Servings: 2

Ingredients

- o Turkey breast – 4 slices, cooked
- o Red bell pepper – 1/2, sliced

- Eggs – 2
- Small avocado – 1, peeled, pitted and sliced
- Salsa – 2 tbsp.
- Salt and black pepper to taste
- Mozzarella cheese – 1/8 cup, grated
- Tortillas for serving

Method

1. In a bowl, whisk the eggs with salt and pepper. Pour them in a pan and place in the air fryers basket.
2. Cook at 400F for 5 minutes. Remove from the fryer and transfer eggs to a plate.
3. Arrange tortillas on a working surface. Distribute the eggs, turkey meat, bell pepper, cheese, salsa and avocado on them.
4. Roll the burritos. Line the air fryer basket with tin foil and place the burritos on it.
5. Heat up the burritos at 300F for 3 minutes.
6. Serve.

Nutritional Facts Per Serving

- Calories: 349
- Fat: 23g
- Carb: 20g

- Protein: 21g

Breakfast Bread Pudding

| Prep time: 10 minutes | Cook time: 22 minutes | Servings: 4 |

Ingredients

- White bread – ½ pound, cubed
- Milk – ¾ cup
- Water – ¾ cup
- Cornstarch – 2 tsp.
- Apple – ½ cup, peeled, cored and chopped
- Honey – 5 tbsp.
- Vanilla extract – 1 tsp.
- Cinnamon powder – 2 tsp.
- Flour – 1 1/3 cup
- Brown sugar – 3/5 cup
- Soft butter – 3 ounces

Method

1. In a bowl, mix bread, apple, cornstarch, vanilla, cinnamon, honey, milk and water. Whisk well.
2. In another bowl, mix butter, sugar and flour, and mix well.

3. Press half of the crumble mixture on the bottom of the air fryer, add bread and apple mixture, then add the rest of the crumble and cook at 350F for 22 minutes.
4. Divide bread pudding on plates and serve.

Nutritional Facts Per Serving

- Calories: 261
- Fat: 7g
- Carb: 8g
- Protein: 5g

Breakfast Fish Tacos

| Prep time: 10 minutes | Cook time: 13 minutes | Servings: 4 |

Ingredients

- Big tortillas – 4
- Red bell pepper – 1, chopped
- Yellow onion – 1, chopped
- Corn – 1 cup
- Whitefish fillets – 4, skinless and boneless
- Salsa – ½ cup
- Mixed romaine lettuce, spinach and radicchio – 1 handful

- Parmesan – 4 tbsp., grated

Method

1. Put fish fillets in the air fryer and cook at 350F for 6 minutes.
2. Meanwhile, heat up a pan over medium-high heat; add corn, onion and bell pepper. Stir-fry for 2 minutes.
3. Arrange tortillas on a working surface. Distribute fish fillets and spread salsa over them; add mixed veggies and mixed greens, and finally sprinkle parmesan on each.
4. Roll the tacos, place them in the preheated air fryer and cook at 350F for 6 minutes more.
5. Arrange fish tacos on plates and serve.

Nutritional Facts Per Serving

- Calories: 200
- Fat: 3g
- Carb: 9g
- Protein: 5g

Shrimp Frittata

Prep time: 10 minutes	Cook time: 15 minutes	Servings: 4

Ingredients

- Eggs – 4
- Basil – ½ tsp., dried
- Cooking spray
- Salt and black pepper to taste
- Rice – ½ cup, cooked
- Shrimp – ½ cup, cooked, peeled, deveined and chopped
- Baby spinach – ½ cup, chopped
- Monterey jack cheese – ½ cup, grated

Method

1. In a bowl, mix eggs with basil, pepper and salt. Whisk well.
2. Grease your air fryers pan with cooking spray and add rice, shrimp and spinach.
3. Add egg mixture, sprinkle cheese all over and cook in the air fryer at 350F for 10 minutes.
4. Serve.

Nutritional Facts Per Serving

- Calories: 162
- Fat: 6g
- Carb: 8g

- Protein: 4g

Tuna Sandwiches

| Prep time: 10 minutes | Cook time: 5 minutes | Servings: 4 |

Ingredients

- Canned tuna – 16 ounces, drained
- Mayonnaise – ¼ cup
- Mustard – 2 tbsp.
- Lemon juice – 1 tbsp.
- Green onions – 2, chopped
- English muffins – 3, halved
- Butter – 3 tbsp.
- Provolone cheese – 6

Method

1. In a bowl, mix mayo, tuna, lemon juice, mustard and green onions.
2. Grease muffin halves with butter. Place them in the preheated air fryer and bake at 350F for 4 minutes.
3. Spread tuna mixture on muffin halves, top each with provolone cheese.
4. Return sandwiches to air fryer and cook them for 4 minutes.

5. Serve.

Nutritional Facts Per Serving

- Calories: 182
- Fat: 4g
- Carb: 8g
- Protein: 6g

Chapter 3: Lunch Recipes

Vegetable Egg Rolls

Prep time: 15 minutes	Cook time: 10 minutes	Servings: 8

Ingredients

- Chopped mushrooms – ½ cup
- Grated carrots – ½ cup
- Chopped zucchini – ½ cup
- Green onions – 2, chopped
- Low-sodium soy sauce – 2 tbsp.
- Egg roll wrappers – 8
- Cornstarch – 1 tbsp.
- Egg – 1, beaten

Method

1. In a bowl, combine the soy sauce, green onions, zucchini, carrots and mushrooms, and stir together.
2. Top each egg roll wrapper with 3 tbsp. of the vegetable mixture.
3. In a small bowl, combine egg and cornstarch and mix well. Brush some of this mixture on the edges of the egg roll wrappers.
4. Roll up the wrappers, enclosing the vegetable filling. Brush some of the egg mixtures on the outside of the egg rolls to seal.

5. Air-fry at 390F for 7 to 10 minutes, or until the egg rolls are brown and crunchy.

Nutritional Facts Per Serving

- Calories: 112
- Fat: 1g
- Carb: 21g
- Protein: 4g

Veggie Toast

Prep time: 10 minutes	Cook time: 15 minutes	Servings: 4

Ingredients

- Red bell pepper – 1, cut into thin strips
- Cremini mushrooms – 1 cup, sliced
- Yellow squash – 1, chopped
- Green onions – 2, sliced
- Olive oil – 1 tbsp.
- Bread – 4 slices
- Butter – 2 tbsp. soft
- Goat cheese – ½ cup, crumbled

Method

1. In a bowl, mix red bell pepper with oil, green onions, squash and mushrooms. Toss.
2. Transfer to the air fryer and cook at 350F for 10 minutes. Shake the air fryer basket once and transfer to a bowl.
3. Spread butter on bread slices and place them in the air fryer.
4. Cook them at 350F for 5 minutes.
5. Distribute vegetable mixture on each bread slice.
6. Top with crumbled cheese and serve.

Nutritional Facts Per Serving

- Calories: 152
- Fat: 3g
- Carb: 7g
- Protein: 2g

Stuffed Mushrooms

Prep time: 10 minutes	Cook time: 20 minutes	Servings: 4

Ingredients

- Big Portobello mushroom caps – 4

- Olive oil – 1 tbsp.
- Ricotta cheese – ¼ cup
- Parmesan – 5 tbsp. grated
- Spinach – 1 cup, torn
- Bread crumbs – 1/3 cup
- Rosemary – ¼ tsp. chopped

Method

1. Rub mushroom caps with oil. Place them in the air fryer basket and cook at 350F for 2 minutes.
2. Meanwhile, in a bowl, mix half of the parmesan with bread crumbs, rosemary, spinach and ricotta. Stir well.
3. Stuff mushrooms with this mixture, and sprinkle the rest of the parmesan on top.
4. Cook in the air fryer basket at 350F for 10 minutes.
5. Serve.

Nutritional Facts Per Serving

- Calories: 152
- Fat: 4g
- Carb: 9g
- Protein: 5g

Lunch Pizzas

| Prep time: 10 minutes | Cook time: 7 minutes | Servings: 4 |

Ingredients

- Pitas – 4
- Olive oil – 1 tbsp.
- Pizza sauce – ¾ cup
- Jarred mushrooms – 4 ounces, sliced
- Basil – ½ tsp. dried
- Green onions – 2, chopped
- Mozzarella – 2 cup, grated
- Grape tomatoes – 1 cup, sliced

Method

1. Spread pizza sauce on each pita bread, sprinkle green onions and basil, distribute mushrooms and top with cheese.
2. Arrange pita pizzas in the air fryer and cook them at 400F for 7 minutes.
3. Top each pizza with tomato sauces, divide among plates, and serve.

Nutritional Facts Per Serving

- Calories: 200
- Fat: 4g
- Carb: 7g

- Protein: 3g

Tuna and Zucchini Tortillas

| Prep time: 10 minutes | Cook time: 10 minutes | Servings: 4 |

Ingredients

- Corn tortillas – 4
- Butter – 4 tbsp. soft
- Canned tuna – 6 ounces, drained
- Zucchini – 1 cup, shredded
- Mayonnaise – 1/3 cup
- Mustard – 2 tbsp.
- Cheddar cheese – 1 cup, grated

Method

1. Spread butter on tortillas.
2. Place them in the air fryer basket and cook at 400F for 3 minutes.
3. Meanwhile, in a bowl, mix tuna with mustard, mayo and zucchini, and stir.
4. Distribute this mixture on each tortilla, top with cheese and roll tortillas.
5. Place them in the air fryer basket and cook at 400F for 4 minutes more.
6. Serve.

Nutritional Facts Per Serving

- Calories: 162
- Fat: 4g
- Carb: 9g
- Protein: 4g

Squash Fritters

Prep time: 10 minutes	Cook time: 7 minutes	Servings: 4

Ingredients

- Cream cheese – 3 ounces
- Egg – 1, whisked
- Oregano – ½ tsp. dried
- Salt and pepper to taste
- Yellow summer squash – 1, grated
- Carrot – 1/3 cup
- Bread crumbs – 2/3 cup
- Olive oil – 2 tbsp.

Method

1. In a bowl, mix cream cheese with squash, carrot, breadcrumbs, egg, oregano, salt and pepper.

2. Shape medium patties out of this mixture and brush them with oil.
3. Place the patties in the air fryer and cook at 400F for 7 minutes.
4. Serve.

Nutritional Facts Per Serving

- Calories: 200
- Fat: 4g
- Carb: 8g
- Protein: 6g

Lunch Shrimp Croquettes

Prep time: 10 minutes	Cook time: 8 minutes	Servings: 4

Ingredients

- Shrimp – 2/3 pound, cooked, peeled, deveined and chopped
- Bread crumbs – 1 ½ cups
- Egg – 1, whisked
- Lemon juice – 2 tbsp.
- Green onions – 3, chopped
- Basil – ½ tsp., dried

- Salt and black pepper to taste
- Olive oil – 2 tbsp.

Method

1. In a bowl, mix half of the bread crumbs with lemon juice and egg, and stir well.
2. Add shrimp, salt, pepper, basil and green onions. Stir well.
3. In another bowl, mix the rest of the bread crumbs with the oil and toss well.
4. Shape round balls out of the shrimp mixture, dredge them in bread crumbs.
5. Place them in the preheated air fryer and cook for 8 minutes, at 400F.
6. Serve.

Nutritional Facts Per Serving

- Calories: 142
- Fat: 4g
- Carb: 9g
- Protein: 4g

Shrimp Pancake

| Prep time: 10 minutes | Cook time: 10 minutes | Servings: 2 |

Ingredients

- Butter – 1 tbsp.
- Eggs – 3, whisked
- Flour – ½ cup
- Milk – ½ cup
- Salsa – 1 cup
- Small shrimp – 1 cup, peeled and deveined

Method

1. Preheat the air fryer at 400F.
2. Add fryer pan, add 1 tbsp. butter and melt it.
3. Mix eggs with milk and flour in a bowl. Whisk well, pour into the air fryer pan, and spread.
4. Cook at 350F for 12 minutes and transfer to a plate.
5. Mix shrimp and salsa in a bowl.
6. Stir and serve pancake with this on the side.

Nutritional Facts Per Serving

- Calories: 200
- Fat: 6g
- Carb: 12g
- Protein: 4g

Chicken Sandwiches

| Prep time: 10 minutes | Cook time: 10 minutes | Servings: 4 |

Ingredients

- Chicken breasts – 2, skinless, boneless and cubed
- Red onion – 1, chopped
- Red bell pepper – 1, sliced
- Italian seasoning – ½ cup
- Thyme – ½ tsp., dried
- Butter lettuce – 2 cups, torn
- Pita pockets – 4
- Cherry tomatoes – 1 cup, halved
- Olive oil – 1 tbsp.

Method

1. In the air fryer, mix chicken with oil, Italian seasoning, bell pepper, onion, then toss and cook at 380F for 10 minutes.
2. Transfer chicken mixture to a bowl, add cherry tomatoes, butter lettuce and thyme. Toss well.
3. Stuff pita pockets with this mixture and serve.

Nutritional Facts Per Serving

- Calories: 126
- Fat: 4g

- Carb: 14g
- Protein: 4g

Hot Bacon Sandwiches

| Prep time: 10 minutes | Cook time: 7 minutes | Servings: 4 |

Ingredients

- BBQ sauce – 1/3 cup
- Honey – 2 tbsp.
- Bacon slices – 8, cooked and cut into thirds
- Red bell pepper – 1, sliced
- Yellow bell pepper – 1, sliced
- Pita pockets – 3, halved
- Butter lettuce leaves – 1 ¼ cup, torn
- Tomatoes – 2, sliced

Method

1. Mix BBQ sauce with honey in a bowl and whisk well.
2. Brush bacon and all bell peppers with this mixture.
3. Place them in the air fryer and cook at 350F for 4 minutes.
4. Shake fryer and cook them for 2 minutes more.
5. Stuff pita pockets with bacon mixture.
6. Also, stuff with lettuce and tomatoes.

7. Spread the rest of the BBQ sauce on the stuffed pita pockets and serve for lunch.

Nutritional Facts Per Serving

- Calories: 186
- Fat: 6g
- Carb: 14g
- Protein: 4g

Buttermilk Chicken

Prep time: 10 minutes	Cook time: 18 minutes	Servings: 4

Ingredients

- Chicken thighs – 1 ½ pounds
- Buttermilk – 2 cups
- Salt and black pepper to taste
- Cayenne pepper – 1 pinch
- White flour – 2 cups
- Baking powder – 1 tbsp.
- Sweet paprika – 1 tbsp.

- Garlic powder – 1 tbsp.

Method

1. In a bowl, mix buttermilk, chicken thighs, salt, pepper and cayenne. Coat well and marinate for 6 hours.
2. In another bowl, mix flour with garlic powder, baking powder and paprika.
3. Drain chicken thighs, dredge them in the flour mixture. Arrange them in the air fryer and cook at 360F for 8 minutes.
4. Flip chicken pieces. Cook for 10 more minutes. Arrange on a platter and serve.

Nutritional Facts Per Serving

- Calories: 200
- Fat: 3g
- Carb: 14g
- Protein: 4g

Macaroni and Cheese

Prep time: 10 minutes	Cook time: 30 minutes	Servings: 3

Ingredients

- Macaroni – 1 ½ cups
- Cooking spray
- Heavy cream – ½ cup
- Chicken stock – 1 cup
- Cheddar cheese – ¾ cup, shredded
- Mozzarella cheese – ½ cup, shredded
- Parmesan – ¼ cup, shredded
- Salt and black pepper to taste

Method

1. Spray a pan with cooking spray.
2. Add macaroni, salt, pepper, parmesan, mozzarella, cheddar cheese, stock and heavy cream. Mix well.
3. Cook in the air fryer for 30 minutes.
4. Serve.

Nutritional Facts Per Serving

- Calories: 341
- Fat: 7g
- Carb: 18g
- Protein: 4g

Fish and Chips

| Prep time: 10 minutes | Cook time: 12 minutes | Servings: 2 |

Ingredients

- Medium cod fillets – 2, skinless and boneless
- Salt and black pepper to taste
- Buttermilk – ¼ cup
- Kettle chips – 3 cups, cooked

Method

1. In a bowl, mix fish with buttermilk, salt and pepper. Toss and set aside for 5 minutes.
2. Crush chips in a food processor and spread them on a plate.
3. Add fish and press well on all sides.
4. Transfer fish on the air fryer basket and cook at 400F for 12 minutes.
5. Serve.

Nutritional Facts Per Serving

- Calories: 271
- Fat: 7g

- Carb: 14g
- Protein: 4g

Delicious Beef Cubes

Prep time: 10 minutes	Cook time: 12 minutes	Servings: 4

Ingredients

- Sirloin – 1 pound, cubed
- Jarred pasta sauce – 16 ounces
- Bread crumbs – 1 ½ cups
- Olive oil – 2 tbsp.
- Marjoram – ½ tsp. dried
- White rice, cooked

Method

1. In a bowl, mix beef cubes with pasta sauce and toss well.
2. In another bowl, mix bread crumbs with marjoram and oil, and stir well.
3. Dip beef cubes in this mixture, place them in the air fryer and cook at 360F for 12 minutes.
4. Serve with white rice.

Nutritional Facts Per Serving

- Calories: 271
- Fat: 6g
- Carb: 18g
- Protein: 12g

Pasta Salad

| Prep time: 10 minutes | Cook time: 12 minutes | Servings: 6 |

Ingredients

- Zucchini – 1, sliced in half and roughly chopped
- Range bell pepper – 1, roughly chopped
- Green bell pepper – 1, roughly chopped
- Red onion – 1, roughly chopped
- Brown mushrooms – 4 ounces, halved
- Salt and black pepper to taste
- Italian seasoning – 1 tsp.
- Penne rigate – 1 pound, cooked
- Cherry tomatoes – 1 cup, halved

- Kalamata olives – ½ cup, pitted and halved
- Olive oil – ¼ cup
- Balsamic vinegar – 3 tbsp.
- Basil – 2 tbsp., chopped

Method

1. In a bowl, combine oil, seasoning, pepper, salt, red onion, green bell pepper, orange bell pepper, mushrooms and zucchini. Mix well.
2. Cook in the air fryer at 380F for 12 minutes.
3. In a bowl, mix the penne pasta with the cooked veggies, basil, vinegar, olive and cherry tomatoes. Toss and serve.

Nutritional Facts Per Serving

- Calories: 200
- Fat: 5g
- Carb: 10g
- Protein: 6g

Chapter 4: Side Dish Recipes

Potato Wedges

| Prep time: 10 minutes | Cook time: 25 minutes | Servings: 4 |

Ingredients

- Potatoes – 2, cut into wedges
- Olive oil – 1 tbsp.
- Salt and black pepper to taste
- Sour cream – 3 tbsp.
- Sweet chili sauce – 2 tbsp.

Method

1. In a bowl, mix potato wedges with oil, salt and pepper. Toss well.
2. Place into the air fryer basket and cook at 360F for 25 minutes. Flip once.
3. Arrange potato wedges on plates.
4. Drizzle with chili sauce and sour cream all over and serve them as a side dish.

Nutritional Facts Per Serving

- Calories: 171
- Fat: 8g

- Carb: 18g
- Protein: 7g

Mushroom Side Dish

Prep time: 10 minutes	Cook time: 8 minutes	Servings: 4

Ingredients

- Button mushrooms – 10, stems removed
- Italian seasoning – 1 tbsp.
- Salt and black pepper to taste
- Cheddar cheese – 2 tbsp., grated
- Olive oil – 1 tbsp.
- Mozzarella – 2 tbsp., grated
- Dill – 1 tbsp., chopped

Method

1. In a bowl, combine mushrooms with oil, seasoning, dill, salt and pepper. Mix well.
2. Arrange mushrooms in the air fryer basket, sprinkle mozzarella and cheddar on each and cook them at 360F for 8 minutes.
3. Divide among plates and serve.

Nutritional Facts Per Serving

- Calories: 241
- Fat: 7g
- Carb: 14g
- Protein: 6g

Sweet Potato Fries

Prep time: 10 minutes	Cook time: 20 minutes	Servings: 2

Ingredients

- Sweet potatoes – 2, peeled and cut into medium fries
- Salt and black pepper to taste
- Olive oil – 2 tbsp.
- Curry powder – ½ tsp.
- Coriander – ¼ tsp. ground
- Ketchup – ¼ cup
- Mayonnaise – 2 tbsp.
- Cumin – ½ tsp. ground
- Ginger powder – 1 pinch
- Cinnamon powder – 1 pinch

Method

1. In the air fryer basket, mix sweet potato fries with salt, pepper, coriander, curry powder and oil. Toss well.
2. Cook at 370F for 20 minutes. Flip once.

3. Meanwhile, in a bowl, mix ketchup with cinnamon, ginger, cumin and mayo. Whisk well.
4. Divide fries among plates. Drizzle ketchup mixture over them and serve.

Nutritional Facts Per Serving

- Calories: 200
- Fat: 5g
- Carb: 9g
- Protein: 7g

Corn with Lime and Cheese

Prep time: 10 minutes	Cook time: 15 minutes	Servings: 2

Ingredients

- Corns on the cob – 2, husks removed
- A drizzle of olive oil
- Feta cheese – ½ cup, grated
- Sweet paprika – 2 tsp.
- Juice from 2 limes

Method

1. Rub corn with oil and paprika.

2. Place in the air fryer basket and cook at 400F for 15 minutes. Flip once.
3. Divide corn among plates, sprinkle cheese on top.
4. Drizzle with lime juice and serve.

Nutritional Facts Per Serving

- Calories: 200
- Fat: 5g
- Carb: 6g
- Protein: 6g

Brussels Sprouts Side Dish

| Prep time: 10 minutes | Cook time: 15 minutes | Servings: 4 |

Ingredients

- Brussels sprouts – 1 pound, trimmed and halved
- Salt and black pepper to taste
- Olive oil – 6 tsp.
- Thyme – ½ tsp., chopped
- Mayonnaise – ½ cup
- Roasted garlic – 2 tbsp., crushed

Method

1. Mix Brussels sprouts with oil, salt and pepper in the air fryer basket and toss well.
2. Cook them at 390F for 15 minutes.
3. Meanwhile, in a bowl, mix mayo, thyme and garlic, and whisk well.
4. Divide Brussels sprouts among plates, drizzle with garlic sauce all over and serve.

Nutritional Facts Per Serving

- Calories: 172
- Fat: 6g
- Carb: 12g
- Protein: 6g

Creamy Potato

Prep time: 10 minutes	Cook time: 1 hour 20 minutes	Servings: 2

Ingredients

- Big potato – 1
- Bacon strips – 2, cooked and chopped
- Olive oil – 1 tsp.
- Cheddar cheese – 1/3 cup, shredded
- Green onions – 1 tbsp. chopped

- Salt and black pepper to taste
- Butter – 1 tbsp.
- Heavy cream – 2 tbsp.

Method

1. Rub potato with oil, season with salt and pepper.
2. Place in the preheated air fryer and cook at 400F for 30 minutes.
3. Flip potato and cook for 30 minutes more.
4. Transfer to a cutting board. Cool and slice in half lengthwise and scoop pulp into a bowl.
5. Add salt, pepper, green onions, heavy cream, butter, cheese and bacon. Stir well and stuff potato skins with this mixture.
6. Return potato to the air fryer and cook them at 400F for 20 minutes.
7. Divide among plates and serve as a side dish.

Nutritional Facts Per Serving

- Calories: 172
- Fat: 5g
- Carb: 9g
- Protein: 4g

Green Beans

Prep time: 10 minutes	Cook time: 25 minutes	Servings: 4

Ingredients

- Green beans – 1 ½ pounds, trimmed and steamed for 2 minutes
- Salt and black pepper to taste
- Shallots – ½ pound, chopped
- Almonds – ¼ cup, toasted
- Olive oil – 2 tbsp.

Method

1. Mix green beans with oil, almonds, shallots, salt and pepper in the air fryer basket. Toss well and cook at 400F for 25 minutes.
2. Divide among plates and serve.

Nutritional Facts Per Serving

- Calories: 152
- Fat: 3g
- Carb: 7g
- Protein: 4g

armesan Mushrooms

| Prep time: 10 minutes | Cook time: 15 minutes | Servings: 3 |

Ingredients

- Button mushroom caps – 9
- Cream cracker slices – 3, crumbled
- Egg white – 1
- Parmesan – 2 tbsp., grated
- Italian seasoning – 1 tsp.
- Salt and black pepper
- Butter – 1 tbsp., melted

Method

1. Mix crackers with butter, Parmesan, salt, pepper, seasoning and egg white. Stir well and stuff mushrooms with this mixture.
2. Arrange mushrooms in the air fryer basket and cook them at 360F for 15 minutes.
3. Divide among plates and serve.

Nutritional Facts Per Serving

- Calories: 124
- Fat: 4g
- Carb: 7g

- Protein: 3g

Eggplant Side Dish

| Prep time: 10 minutes | Cook time: 10 minutes | Servings: 4 |

Ingredients

- Baby eggplants – 8, scooped in the center and pulp reserved
- Salt and black pepper to taste
- A pinch of oregano, dried
- Green bell pepper – 1, chopped
- Tomato paste – 1 tbsp.
- Coriander – 1 bunch, chopped
- Garlic powder – ½ tsp.
- Olive oil – 1 tbsp.
- Yellow onion – 1, chopped
- Tomato – 1, chopped

Method

1. Heat oil in a pan and add the onion. Stir-fry for 1 minute.
2. Add tomato, coriander, garlic powder, tomato paste, green bell pepper, oregano, eggplant pulp, salt and pepper.
3. Stir-fry for 2 minutes more. Remove from heat and cool.

4. Stuff eggplants with this mixture; place them in the air fryer basket.
5. Cook at 360F for 8 minutes.
6. Divide eggplants among plates and serve.

Nutritional Facts Per Serving

- Calories: 200
- Fat: 3g
- Carb: 12g
- Protein: 4g

Eggplant Fries

| Prep time: 10 minutes | Cook time: 5 minutes | Servings: 4 |

Ingredients

- Cooking spray
- Eggplant – 1, peeled and cut into medium fries
- Milk – 2 tbsp.
- Egg – 1, whisked
- Panko bread crumbs – 2 cups
- Italian cheese – ½ cup, shredded
- Salt and black pepper to taste

Method

1. In a bowl, mix milk with egg, salt and pepper. Whisk well.
2. In another bowl, mix cheese and panko then stir.
3. Dip eggplant fries in the egg mixture, then coat in panko mix.
4. Grease the air fryer basket with cooking spray and place the eggplant fries in it.
5. Cook at 400F for 5 minutes.
6. Serve.

Nutritional Facts Per Serving

- Calories: 162
- Fat: 5g
- Carb: 7g
- Protein: 6g

Cauliflower Cakes

Prep time: 10 minutes	Cook time: 10 minutes	Servings: 6

Ingredients

- Cauliflower rice – 3 ½ cups

- Eggs – 2
- White flour – ¼ cup
- Parmesan – ½ cup, grated
- Salt and black pepper to taste
- Cooking spray

Method

1. In a bowl, mix cauliflower rice with salt and pepper. Stir and squeeze excess water.
2. Transfer cauliflower to another bowl. Add eggs, parmesan, flour, salt and pepper. Mix well and shape into cakes.
3. Grease the air fryer basket with cooking spray.
4. Heat it up at 400F and add cauliflower cakes then cook them for 10 minutes. Flip once.
5. Serve.

Nutritional Facts Per Serving

- Calories: 125
- Fat: 2g
- Carb: 8g
- Protein: 3g

Cheddar Biscuits

| Prep time: 10 minutes | Cook time: 20 minutes | Servings: 8 |

Ingredients

- Self-rising flour – 2 1/3 cups
- Butter – ½ cup plus 1 tbsp., melted
- Sugar – 2 bsp.
- Cheddar cheese – ½ cup, grated
- Buttermilk – 1 1/3 cup
- Flour – 1 cup

Method

1. In a bowl, mix buttermilk, cheddar cheese, sugar, ½ cup butter and self-rising flour. Make a dough.
2. Spread 1-cup flour on a working surface, roll dough, flatten it, cut 8 circles with a cookie cutter and coat them with flour.
3. Line the air fryer basket with tin foil. Add biscuits, brush with melted butter and cook at 380F for 20 minutes.
4. Serve.

Nutritional Facts Per Serving

- Calories: 221
- Fat: 3g
- Carb: 12g
- Protein: 4g

Zucchini Fries

Prep time: 10 minutes	Cook time: 12 minutes	Servings: 4

Ingredients

- Zucchini – 1, cut into medium sticks
- Olive oil – 1 drizzle
- Salt and black pepper to taste
- Eggs – 2, whisked
- Bread crumbs – 1 cup
- Flour – ½ cup

Method

1. In a bowl, add flour and mix with salt and pepper.

2. Put breadcrumbs in another bowl.
3. In a third bowl, mix the egg with salt and pepper.
4. Dredge zucchini fries in flour, then in eggs and in bread crumbs.
5. Grease the air fryer with olive oil.
6. Heat up at 400F. Add zucchini fries and cook them for 12 minutes.
7. Serve.

Nutritional Facts Per Serving

- Calories: 172
- Fat: 3g
- Carb: 7g
- Protein: 3g

Herbed Tomatoes

Prep time: 10 minutes	Cook time: 15 minutes	Servings: 4

Ingredients

- Big tomatoes – 4, halved and inside scooped out
- Salt and black pepper to taste
- Olive oil – 1 tbsp.

- o Garlic – 2 cloves, minced
- o Thyme – ½ tsp., chopped

Method

1. In the air fryer, mix tomatoes with thyme, garlic, oil, salt and pepper.
2. Mix and cook at 390F for 15 minutes.
3. Serve.

Nutritional Facts Per Serving

- o Calories: 112
- o Fat: 1g
- o Carb: 4g
- o Protein: 4g

Creamy Endives

Prep time: 10 minutes	Cook time: 10 minutes	Servings: 6

Ingredients

- Endives – 6, trimmed and halved
- Garlic powder – 1 tsp.
- Greek yogurt – ½ cup
- Curry powder – ½ tsp.
- Salt and black pepper to taste
- Lemon juice – 3 tbsp.

Method

1. In a bowl, mix endives with lemon juice, salt, pepper, curry powder, yogurt and garlic powder. Coat well and set aside for 10 minutes.
2. Cook in the preheated 350F air fryer for 10 minutes.
3. Serve.

Nutritional Facts Per Serving

- Calories: 100
- Fat: 2g
- Carb: 7g
- Protein: 4g

Chapter 5: Snack and Appetizer Recipes

Coconut Chicken Bites

| Prep time: 10 minutes | Cook time: 13 minutes | Servings: 4 |

Ingredients

- Garlic powder – 2 tsp.
- Eggs – 2
- Salt and black pepper to taste
- Panko bread crumbs – ¾ cup
- Coconut – ¾ cup, shredded
- Cooking spray
- Chicken tenders – 8

Method

1. In a bowl, mix eggs with garlic powder, salt and pepper, and whisk well.
2. In another bowl, mix coconut with panko and stir well.
3. Dip chicken tenders in the egg mixture and then coat well with coconut mixture.
4. Spray chicken bits with cooking spray.
5. Place them in the air fryer basket and cook at 350F for 10 minutes.
6. Serve.

Nutritional Facts Per Serving

- Calories: 252
- Fat: 4g
- Carb: 14g
- Protein: 24g

Buffalo Cauliflower Snack

| Prep time: 10 minutes | Cook time: 15 minutes | Servings: 4 |

Ingredients

- Cauliflower florets – 4 cups
- Panko bread crumbs – 1 cup
- Butter – ¼ cup, melted
- Buffalo sauce – ¼ cup
- Mayonnaise for serving

Method

1. In a bowl, mix butter and buffalo sauce, and whisk well.
2. Dip cauliflower florets in the mixture and coat them in panko bread crumbs.
3. Place them in the air fryer basket and cook at 350F for 15 minutes.
4. Serve.

Nutritional Facts Per Serving

- Calories: 241
- Fat: 4g
- Carb: 8g
- Protein: 4g

Banana Snack

| Prep time: 10 minutes | Cook time: 5 minutes | Servings: 8 |

Ingredients

- Peanut butter – ¼ cup
- Chocolate chips – ¾ cup
- Banana – 1, peeled and sliced in 16 pieces
- Vegetable oil – 1 tbsp.

Other

- 16 baking cups crust

Method

1. Melt the chocolate chips in a small pot over low heat or in the microwave.
2. In a bowl, mix coconut oil with peanut butter and whisk well.

3. Spoon 1 tsp. chocolate mix in a cup, add 1 slice of banana and top with 1 tsp. butter mix.
4. Repeat with the rest of the cups; place them all into a dish that fits the air fryer.
5. Cook at 320F for 5 minutes.
6. Cool, freeze and serve.

Nutritional Facts Per Serving

- Calories: 70
- Fat: 4g
- Carb: 10g
- Protein: 1g

Apple Snack

| Prep time: 10 minutes | Cook time: 5 minutes | Servings: 4 |

Ingredients

- Big apples – 3, cored, peeled and cubed
- Lemon juice – 2 tsp.
- Pecans – ¼ cup, chopped
- Dark chocolate chips – ½ cup
- Clean caramel sauce – ½ cup

Method

1. Mix apples and lemon juice in a bowl.
2. Place in a dish that fits in the air fryer.
3. Add pecans and chocolate chips, then drizzle with caramel sauce. Toss to coat.
4. Cook at 320F for 5 minutes in the air fryer.
5. Serve.

Nutritional Facts Per Serving

- Calories: 200
- Fat: 4g
- Carb: 20g
- Protein: 3g

Shrimp Muffins

Prep time: 10 minutes	Cook time: 26 minutes	Servings: 6

Ingredients

- Spaghetti squash – 1, peeled and halved
- Mayonnaise – 2 tbsp.
- Mozzarella 1 cup, shredded
- Shrimp – 8 ounces, peeled, cooked and chopped
- Panko – 1 ½ cups
- Parsley flakes – 1 tsp.

- Garlic clove – 1, minced
- Salt and black pepper to taste
- Cooking spray

Method

1. Place squash halves in the air fryer.
2. Cook at 350F for 16 minutes. Cool and scrape flesh into a bowl.
3. Add mozzarella, mayo, shrimp, panko, parsley flakes, pepper and salt. Mix well.
4. Spray a muffin tray with cooking spray and distribute squash and shrimp mixture in each cup.
5. Place in the air fryer and cook at 360F for 10 minutes.
6. Serve.

Nutritional Facts Per Serving

- Calories: 60
- Fat: 2g
- Carb: 4g
- Protein: 4g

Zucchini Cakes

| Prep time: 10 minutes | Cook time: 12 minutes | Servings: 12 |

Ingredients

- Cooking spray
- Dill – ½ cup, chopped
- Egg – 1
- Whole wheat flour – ½ cup
- Salt and black pepper to taste
- Yellow onion – 1, chopped
- Garlic cloves – 2, minced
- Zucchinis – 3, grated

Method

1. In a bowl, combine zucchinis with dill, egg, salt, pepper, flour, onion and garlic. Mix well.
2. Make small patties with the mixture and spray them with cooking spray.
3. Place them in the air fryer basket and cook at 370F for 6 minutes on each side.
4. Serve.

Nutritional Facts Per Serving

- Calories: 60

- o Fat: 1g
- o Carb: 6g
- o Protein: 2g

Pesto Crackers

Prep time: 10 minutes	Cook time: 17 minutes	Servings: 6

Ingredients

- o Baking powder – ½ tsp.
- o Salt and black pepper to taste
- o Flour – 1 ¼ cups
- o Basil – ¼ tsp., dried
- o Garlic – 1 clove, minced
- o Basil pesto - 2 tbsp.
- o Butter – 3 tbsp.

Method

1. Mix butter, pesto, basil, cayenne, garlic, flour, baking powder, salt and pepper in a bowl and make a dough.
2. Spread the dough on a lined baking sheet.
3. Bake in the air fryer at 325F for 17 minutes.
4. Cool and cut into crackers. Serve.

Nutritional Facts Per Serving

- Calories: 200
- Fat: 20g
- Carb: 4g
- Protein: 7g

Pumpkin Muffins

Prep time: 10 minutes	Cook time: 15 minutes	Servings: 18

Ingredients

- Butter – ¼ cup
- Pumpkin puree – ¾ cup
- Flaxseed meal – 2 tbsp.
- Flour – ¼ cup
- Sugar – ½ cup
- Nutmeg – ½ tsp., ground
- Cinnamon powder – 1 tsp.
- Baking powder – ½ tsp.
- Egg – 1
- Baking powder – ½ tsp.

Method

1. Mix butter, pumpkin puree and egg in a bowl, and blend well.
2. Add cinnamon, nutmeg, baking powder, baking soda, sugar, flour and flaxseed meal.
3. Spoon this into a muffin pan.
4. Bake in the air fryer at 350F for 15 minutes.
5. Serve.

Nutritional Facts Per Serving

- Calories: 50
- Fat: 3g
- Carb: 2g
- Protein: 2g

Zucchini Chips

Prep time: 10 minutes	Cook time: 1 hour	Servings: 6

Ingredients

- Zucchinis – 3, thinly sliced
- Salt and black pepper to taste
- Olive oil – 2 tbsp.
- Balsamic vinegar – 2 tbsp.

Method

1. Mix vinegar, oil, salt and pepper, and whisk well.
2. Add zucchini slices and toss to coat.
3. Cook in the air fryer at 200F for 1 hour. Shake once.
4. Serve.

Nutritional Facts Per Serving

- Calories: 40
- Fat: 3g
- Carb: 3g
- Protein: 7g

Beef Jerky

Prep time: 2 hours	Cook time: 1 hour 30 minutes	Servings: 6

Ingredients

- Soy sauce – 2 cups
- Worcestershire sauce – ½ cup
- Black peppercorns – 2 tbsp.
- Black pepper – 2 tbsp.
- Beef round – 2 pounds, sliced

Method

1. In a bowl, mix Worcestershire sauce, black pepper, black peppercorns and soy sauce, and whisk well.
2. Add beef slices. Coat and keep in the refrigerator for 6 hours to marinate.
3. Cook in the air fryer at 370F for 1 hour and 30 minutes.
4. Transfer to a bowl and serve.

Nutritional Facts Per Serving

- Calories: 300
- Fat: 12g
- Carb: 3g
- Protein: 8g

Salmon Party Patties

Prep time: 10 minutes	Cook time: 22 minutes	Servings: 4

Ingredients

- Big potatoes – 3, boiled, drained and mashed
- Big salmon fillet – 1, skinless, boneless
- Parsley – 2 tbsp., chopped

- Dill – 2 tbsp., chopped
- Salt and black pepper to taste
- Egg – 1
- Bread crumbs – 2 tbsp.
- Cooking spray

Method

1. Cook salmon in the air fryer basket at 360F for 10 minutes.
2. Transfer salmon to a cutting board. Cool, flake it and put it in a bowl.
3. Add bread crumbs, egg, parsley, dill, salt, pepper and mashed potatoes. Mix and shape 8 patties.
4. Place salmon patties in the air fryer basket and spray with cooking oil.
5. Cook at 360F for 12 minutes. Flip once at the halfway mark.
6. Serve.

Nutritional Facts Per Serving

- Calories: 231
- Fat: 3g
- Carb: 14g

- Protein: 4g

Banana Chips

Prep time: 10 minutes	Cook time: 15 minutes	Servings: 4

Ingredients

- Bananas – 4, peeled and sliced
- Salt – 1 pinch
- Turmeric powder – ½ tsp.
- Chaat masala – ½ tsp.
- Olive oil – 1 tsp.

Method

1. In a bowl, mix banana slices with oil, chaat masala, turmeric and salt. Toss and set aside for 10 minutes.
2. Cook in the air fryer at 360F for 15 minutes. Flip them once.
3. Serve.

Nutritional Facts Per Serving

- Calories: 121

- o Fat: 1g
- o Carb: 3g
- o Protein: 3g

Spring Rolls

| Prep time: 10 minutes | Cook time: 25 minutes | Servings: 8 |

Ingredients

- o Green cabbage – 2 cups, shredded
- o Yellow onions – 2, chopped
- o Carrot – 1 grated
- o Chili pepper – ½, minced
- o Ginger – 1 tbsp.
- o Garlic – 3 cloves, minced
- o Sugar – 1 tsp.
- o Salt and black pepper to taste
- o Soy sauce – 1 tsp.
- o Olive oil – 2 tbsp.
- o Spring roll sheets – 10

- Corn flour – 2 tbsp.
- Water – 2 tbsp.

Method

1. Heat oil in a pan over medium heat. Add soy sauce, pepper, salt, sugar, garlic, ginger, chili pepper, carrots, onions and cabbage. Stir-fry for 2 to 3 minutes. Remove from heat and let it cool down.
2. Cut spring roll sheets in squares, distribute cabbage mixture on each and roll them.
3. In a bowl, mix corn flour with water, stir well and seal spring rolls with this mixture.
4. Place spring rolls in the air fryer basket and cook at 360F for 10 minutes.
5. Flip roll and cook them for 10 minutes more.
6. Serve.

Nutritional Facts Per Serving

- Calories: 214
- Fat: 4g
- Carb: 12g
- Protein: 4g

Crab Sticks

| Prep time: 10 minutes | Cook time: 12 minutes | Servings: 4 |

Ingredients

- Crabsticks – 10, halved
- Sesame oil – 2 tsp.
- Cajun seasoning – 2 tsp.

Method

1. Put crab sticks in a bowl. Add seasoning and sesame oil. Toss and place in the air fryer basket. Cook at 350F for 12 minutes.
2. Serve.

Nutritional Facts Per Serving

- Calories: 110
- Fat: 0g
- Carb: 4g
- Protein: 2g

Chickpeas Snack

Prep time: 10 minutes	Cook time: 10 minutes	Servings: 4

Ingredients

- Canned chickpeas – 15 ounces, drained
- Cumin – ½ tsp. ground
- Olive oil – 1 tbsp.
- Smoked paprika – 1 tsp.
- Salt and black pepper to taste

Method

1. In a bowl, mix chickpeas with oil, salt, pepper, paprika and cumin. Toss to coat and place in the air fryer basket.
2. Cook at 390F for 10 minutes.
3. Serve.

Nutritional Facts Per Serving

- Calories: 140
- Fat: 1g
- Carb: 20g

- Protein: 6g

Chapter 6: Fish and Seafood Recipes

Tasty Cod

Prep time: 10 minutes	Cook time: 12 minutes	Servings: 4

Ingredients

- Cod fillets – 2 (7-ounces each)
- Sesame oil – 1 drizzle
- Salt and black pepper to taste
- Water – 1 cup
- Dark soy sauce – 1 tsp.
- Light soy sauce – 4 tbsp.
- Sugar – 1 tbsp.
- Olive oil – 3 tbsp.
- Ginger – 4 slices
- Spring onions – 3, chopped
- Coriander – 2 tbsp., chopped

Method

1. Season fish with sesame oil, salt and pepper. Rub well and set aside for 10 minutes.
2. Cook in the air fryer at 356F for 12 minutes.
3. Meanwhile, heat up a pot with water over medium heat.
4. Add both soy sauces and sugar, stir and bring to a simmer. Remove from heat.

5. Heat olive oil in a pan over medium heat. Add green onions and ginger, stir and cook for a few minutes then remove from heat.
6. Divide fish among plates, top with green onions and ginger.
7. Drizzle with soy sauce mix and sprinkle with coriander.
8. Serve.

Nutritional Facts Per Serving

- Calories: 300
- Fat: 17g
- Carb: 20g
- Protein: 22g

Delicious Catfish

Prep time: 10 minutes	Cook time: 20 minutes	Servings: 4

Ingredients

- Catfish fillets – 4
- Salt and black pepper to taste
- A pinch of sweet paprika
- Parsley – 1 tbsp., chopped
- Lemon juice – 1 tbsp.
- Olive oil – 1 tbsp.

Method

1. Season catfish fillets with oil, paprika, pepper and salt. Rub well.
2. Cook in the air fryer at 400F for 20 minutes. Flip the fish after 10 minutes.
3. Divide fish among plates, drizzle lemon juice all over, sprinkle with parsley and serve.

Nutritional Facts Per Serving

- Calories: 253
- Fat: 6g
- Carb: 26g
- Protein: 22g

Tabasco Shrimp

| Prep time: 10 minutes | Cook time: 10 minutes | Servings: 4 |

Ingredients

- Shrimp – 1 pound, peeled and deveined
- Red pepper flakes – 1 tsp.
- Olive oil – 2 tbsp.
- Tabasco sauce – 1 tsp.

- Water – 2 tbsp.
- Oregano – 1 tsp., dried
- Salt and black pepper to taste
- Dried parsley – ½ tsp.
- Smoked paprika – ½ tsp.

Method

1. In a bowl, mix water, oil, Tabasco sauce, shrimp, paprika, pepper, salt, parsley, oregano and pepper flakes. Coat well.
2. Transfer shrimp to preheated air fryer at 370F and cook for 10 minutes. Shake once.
3. Serve.

Nutritional Facts Per Serving

- Calories: 200
- Fat: 5g
- Carb: 13g
- Protein: 8g

Buttered Shrimp Skewers

| Prep time: 10 minutes | Cook time: 6 minutes | Servings: 2 |

Ingredients

- Shrimps – 8, peeled and deveined
- Garlic – 4 cloves, minced
- Salt and black pepper to taste
- Green bell pepper slices – 8
- Rosemary – 1 tbsp., chopped
- Butter – 1 tbsp., melted

Method

1. In a bowl, mix bell pepper slices, rosemary, pepper, salt, butter, garlic and shrimp. Toss to coat and marinate for 10 minutes.
2. Arrange 2 bell pepper slices and 2 shrimps on a skewer and repeat with the rest of the shrimp and bell pepper pieces.
3. Cook them at 360F for 6 minutes.
4. Serve.

Nutritional Facts Per Serving

- Calories: 140
- Fat: 1g
- Carb: 15g
- Protein: 7g

Asian Salmon

| Prep time: 1 hour | Cook time: 15 minutes | Servings: 2 |

Ingredients

- Salmon fillets – 2 medium
- Light soy sauce – 6 tbsp.
- Mirin – 3 tbsp.
- Water – 1 tsp.
- Honey – 6 tbsp.

Method

1. Mix soy sauce with water, honey and mirin, and whisk well. Add salmon, rub well and marinate in the fridge for 1 hour.
2. Cook at 360F for 15 minutes in the air fryer. Flip once after 7 minutes.
3. Meanwhile, put the soy marinade in a pan, simmer and whisk on medium heat for 2 minutes.
4. Divide salmon among plates. Drizzle marinade all over and serve.

Nutritional Facts Per Serving

- Calories: 300
- Fat: 12g

- o Carb: 13g
- o Protein: 24g

Air Fried Salmon

| Prep time: 1 hour | Cook time: 8 minutes | Servings: 2 |

Ingredients

- o Salmon fillets – 2
- o Lemon juice – 2 tbsp.
- o Salt and black pepper to taste
- o Garlic powder – ½ tsp.
- o Water – 1/3 cup
- o Soy sauce – 1/3 cup
- o Scallions – 3, chopped
- o Brown sugar – 1/3 cup
- o Olive oil – 2 tbsp.

Method

1. In a bowl, mix water, sugar, garlic powder, soy sauce, salt, pepper, oil and lemon juice. Whisk well and add salmon fillets. Coat well and marinate in the refrigerator for 1 hour.
2. Cook salmon in the air fryer at 360F for 8 minutes. Flip once.
3. Divide salmon among plates. Sprinkle scallions on top and serve.

Nutritional Facts Per Serving

- Calories: 300
- Fat: 12g
- Carb: 23g
- Protein: 20g

Lemony Saba Fish

| Prep time: 10 minutes | Cook time: 8 minutes | Servings: 1 |

Ingredients

- Saba fish fillet – 4, boneless
- Salt and black pepper to taste
- Red chili pepper – 3, chopped
- Lemon juice – 2 tbsp.
- Olive oil – 2 tbsp.
- Garlic – 2 tbsp., minced

Method

1. Season fish fillets with salt and pepper, and place in a bowl.
2. Add garlic, chili, oil and lemon juice, and toss to coat.

3. Transfer fish to the air fryer and cook at 360F for 8 minutes. Flip them halfway.
4. Serve.

Nutritional Facts Per Serving

- Calories: 300
- Fat: 4g
- Carb: 15g
- Protein: 15g

Asian Halibut

| Prep time: 30 minutes | Cook time: 10 minutes | Servings: 3 |

Ingredients

- Halibut steaks – 1 pound
- Soy sauce – 2/3 cup
- Sugar – ¼ cup
- Lime juice – 2 tbsp.
- Mirin – ½ cup
- Red pepper flakes – ¼ tsp., crushed
- Orange juice – ¼ cup
- Ginger – ¼ tsp., grated
- Garlic – 1 clove, minced

Method

1. Pour soy sauce in a pan and heat over medium heat.
2. Add garlic, ginger, pepper flakes, orange juice, lime, sugar and mirin.
3. Stir well, bring to a boil and remove from heat.
4. Transfer half of the marinade to a bowl, add halibut, toss to coat and marinate in the refrigerator for 30 minutes.
5. Cook halibut in the air fryer at 390F for 10 minutes. Flip once.
6. Divide halibut steaks among plates, drizzle the rest of the marinade all over and serve.

Nutritional Facts Per Serving

- Calories: 286
- Fat: 5g
- Carb: 14g
- Protein: 23g

Shrimp and Crab Mix

| Prep time: 10 minutes | Cook time: 25 minutes | Servings: 4 |

Ingredients

- Yellow onion – ½ cup, chopped
- Green bell pepper – 1 cup, chopped
- Celery – 1 cup, chopped
- Shrimp – 1 cup, peeled and deveined
- Crabmeat – 1 cup, flaked
- Mayonnaise – 1 cup
- Worcestershire sauce – 1 tsp.
- Salt and black pepper to taste
- Breadcrumbs – 2 tbsp.
- Butter – 1 tbsp., melted
- Sweet paprika – 1 tsp.

Method

1. In a bowl, mix crab meat, shrimp, onion, bell pepper, celery, mayo, salt, pepper and Worcestershire sauce. Transfer to a pan.
2. Add melted butter, paprika and bread crumbs. Coat well and place in the air fryer.
3. Cook at 320F for 25 minutes. Shake once at the halfway mark.
4. Serve.

Nutritional Facts Per Serving

- Calories: 200
- Fat: 13g

- Carb: 17g

- Protein: 19g

Seafood Casserole

Prep time: 10 minutes	Cook time: 40 minutes	Servings: 6

Ingredients

- Butter – 6 tbsp.
- Mushrooms – 2 ounces, chopped
- Green bell pepper – 1 small, chopped
- Celery – 1 stalk, chopped
- Garlic – 2 cloves, minced
- Small yellow onion – 1, chopped
- Salt and black pepper to taste
- Flour – 4 tbsp.
- White wine – ½ cup
- Milk – 1 ½ cups
- Heavy cream – ½ cup
- Sea scallops – 4, sliced
- Haddock – 4 ounces, skinless, boneless and cut into small pieces
- Lobster meat – 4 ounces, cooked and cut into small pieces

- Mustard powder – ½ tsp.
- Lemon juice – 1 tbsp.
- Bread crumbs – 1/3 cup
- Salt and black pepper to taste
- Cheddar cheese – 3 tbsp., grated
- Handful parsley, chopped
- Sweet paprika – 1 tsp.

Method

1. Heat 4 tbsp. butter in a pan over medium-high heat.
2. Add wine, onion, garlic, celery, mushrooms and bell pepper, and cook for 10 minutes.
3. Add milk, cream and flour, stir well and cook for 6 minutes.
4. Add haddock, lobster meat, scallops, mustard powder, salt, pepper and lemon juice, and stir well. Remove from heat and place in a pan.
5. In a bowl, mix the rest of the butter with cheese, paprika and bread crumbs, and sprinkle over seafood mix.
6. Transfer the pan to the air fryer and cook at 360F for 16 minutes.
7. Serve garnished with parsley.

Nutritional Facts Per Serving

- Calories: 270

- Fat: 32g
- Carb: 15g
- Protein: 23g

Trout and Butter Sauce

| Prep time: 10 minutes | Cook time: 10 minutes | Servings: 4 |

Ingredients

- Trout fillets – 4, boneless
- Salt and black pepper to taste
- Lemon zest – 3 tsp., grated
- Chives – 3 tbsp., chopped
- Butter – 6 tbsp.
- Olive oil – 2 tbsp.
- Lemon juice – 2 tsp.

Method

1. Season trout with salt and pepper. Drizzle with oil and rub well.
2. Cook in the air fryer at 360F for 10 minutes. Flip once.
3. Meanwhile, heat up a pan with the butter over medium heat. Add lemon juice, zest, chives, salt and pepper. Whisk well and cook for 2 minutes. Then remove from heat.

4. Divide fish fillets among plates. Drizzle butter sauce all over and serve.

Nutritional Facts Per Serving

- Calories: 300
- Fat: 12g
- Carb: 27g
- Protein: 24g

Creamy Salmon

| Prep time: 10 minutes | Cook time: 10 minutes | Servings: 4 |

Ingredients

- Salmon – 4 fillets, boneless
- Olive oil – 1 tbsp.
- Salt and black pepper to taste
- Cheddar cheese – 1/3 cup, grated
- Mustard – 1 ½ tsp.
- Coconut cream – ½ cup

Method

1. Season salmon with salt and pepper. Drizzle with oil and rub well.
2. In a bowl, mix cheddar, coconut cream, mustard, salt and pepper, and stir well.

3. Transfer salmon to a pan and add coconut cream mixture.
4. Cook in the air fryer at 320F for 10 minutes.
5. Serve.

Nutritional Facts Per Serving

- Calories: 200
- Fat: 6g
- Carb: 17g
- Protein: 20g

Barramundi with Tomato Salsa

Prep time: 10 minutes	Cook time: 8 minutes	Servings: 4

Ingredients

- Barramundi – 2 fillets, boneless
- Olive oil – 1 tbsp. plus 2 tsp.
- Italian seasoning – 2 tsp.
- Green olives – ¼ cup, pitted and chopped
- Cherry tomatoes – ¼ cup, chopped
- Black olives – ¼ cup, chopped
- Lemon zest – 2 tbsp.
- Salt and black pepper to taste
- Parsley – 2 tbsp., chopped

Method

1. Rub fish with salt, pepper, seasoning and 2 tsp. olive oil.
2. Cook in the air fryer at 360F for 8 minutes. Flip them halfway.
3. In a bowl, mix 1 tbsp. olive oil, parsley, lemon zest, lemon juice, salt, pepper, green olives, black olives and tomatoes. Mix well.
4. Divide fish among plates. Add tomato salsa on top and serve.

Nutritional Facts Per Serving

- Calories: 270
- Fat: 4g
- Carb: 18g
- Protein: 27g

Creamy Shrimp and Veggies

Prep time: 10 minutes	Cook time: 30 minutes	Servings: 4

Ingredients

- Mushrooms – 8 ounces, chopped
- Asparagus – 1 bunch, cut into medium pieces

- Shrimp – 1 pound, peeled and deveined
- Salt and black pepper to taste
- Spaghetti squash – 1, cut into halves
- Olive oil – 2 tbsp.
- Italian seasoning – 2 tsp.
- Yellow onion – 1, chopped
- Red pepper flakes -1 tsp., crushed
- Butter – ¼ cup, melted
- Parmesan cheese – 1 cup, grated
- Garlic – 2 cloves, minced
- Heavy cream – 1 cup

Method

1. Cook squash halves in the air fryer at 390F for 17 minutes. Transfer to a cutting board, scoop insides and transfer to a bowl.
2. Bring a pot of lightly salted water to boil. Add asparagus and steam for a couple of minutes. Then remove and place in ice water, drain and set aside.
3. In a pan, heat up oil over medium heat. Add mushrooms and onions, and stir-fry for 7 minutes.
4. Add garlic, parmesan, cream, melted butter, shrimp, asparagus, squash, salt, pepper, seasoning and pepper flakes. Toss and cook in the air fryer at 360F for 6 minutes.
5. Serve.

Nutritional Facts Per Serving

- Calories: 325
- Fat: 6g
- Carb: 14g
- Protein: 13g

Tuna and Chimichurri Sauce

| Prep time: 10 minutes | Cook time: 8 minutes | Servings: 4 |

Ingredients

- Cilantro – ½ cup, chopped
- Olive oil – 1/3 cup plus 2 tbsp.
- Small red onion – 1, chopped
- Balsamic vinegar – 3 tbsp.
- Parsley – 2 tbsp., chopped
- Basil – 2 tbsp., chopped
- Jalapeno pepper – 1, chopped
- Sushi tuna steak – 1 pound
- Salt and black pepper to taste
- Red pepper flakes – 1 tsp.
- Thyme – 1 tsp., chopped
- Garlic – 3 cloves, minced
- Avocados – 2, sliced
- Baby arugula – 6 ounces

Method

1. In a bowl, mix 1/3 cup oil with salt, pepper, thyme, pepper flakes, parsley, garlic, basil, cilantro, onion, vinegar, jalapeno and 1/3 cup oil. Whisk well and set aside.
2. Season tuna with salt and pepper. Rub with the rest of the oil.
3. Cook in the air fryer at 360F for 3 minutes on each side.
4. Mix arugula with half of the chimichurri mixture and toss to coat.
5. Divide arugula among plates. Slice tuna and also divide among plates. Top with the rest of the chimichurri and serve.

Nutritional Facts Per Serving

- Calories: 276
- Fat: 3g
- Carb: 14g
- Protein: 20g

Chapter 7: Poultry Recipes

Creamy Coconut Chicken

| Prep time: 2 hours | Cook time: 25 minutes | Servings: 4 |

Ingredients

- Big chicken legs – 4
- Turmeric powder – 5 tsp.
- Ginger – 2 tbsp., grated
- Salt and black pepper to taste
- Coconut cream – 4 tbsp.

Method

1. In a bowl, mix salt, pepper, ginger, turmeric and cream. Whisk. Add chicken pieces, coat and marinate for 2 hours.
2. Transfer chicken to the preheated air fryer and cook at 370F for 25 minutes.
3. Serve.

Nutritional Facts Per Serving

- Calories: 300
- Fat: 4g

- Carb: 22g
- Protein: 20g

Chinese Chicken Wings

| Prep time: 2 hours | Cook time: 15 minutes | Servings: 6 |

Ingredients

- Chicken wings – 16
- Honey – 2 tbsp.
- Soy sauce – 2 tbsp.
- Salt and black pepper to taste
- White pepper – ¼ tsp.
- Lime juice – 3 tbsp.

Method

1. In a bowl, mix soy sauce, honey, salt, black pepper, lime juice and white pepper. Whisk well.
2. Add chicken pieces and coat well. Marinate in the refrigerator for 2 hours.
3. Cook in the air fryer at 370F for 6 minutes on each side.
4. Increase heat to 400F and cook for 3 minutes more.
5. Serve.

Nutritional Facts Per Serving

- Calories: 372
- Fat: 9g
- Carb: 37g
- Protein: 24g

Herbed Chicken

Prep time: 30 minutes	Cook time: 40 minutes	Servings: 4

Ingredients

- Whole chicken – 1
- Salt and black pepper to taste
- Garlic powder – 1 tsp.
- Onion powder – 1 tsp.
- Thyme – ½ tsp., dried
- Rosemary – 1 tsp., dried
- Lemon juice – 1 tbsp.
- Olive oil – 2 tbsp.

Method

1. Season chicken with salt and pepper. Rub with onion powder, garlic powder, rosemary and thyme. Rub with olive oil and lemon juice, and marinate for 30 minutes.
2. Cook chicken in the air fryer at 360F for 20 minutes on each side.

3. Carve and serve.

Nutritional Facts Per Serving

- Calories: 390
- Fat: 10g
- Carb: 22g
- Protein: 20g

Chicken Parmesan

| Prep time: 10 minutes | Cook time: 15 minutes | Servings: 4 |

Ingredients

- Panko bread crumbs – 2 cups
- Parmesan – ¼ cup, grated
- Garlic powder – ½ tsp.
- White flour – 2 cups
- Egg – 1, whisked
- Chicken cutlets – 1 ½ pounds, skinless and boneless
- Salt and pepper to taste
- Mozzarella - 1 cup, grated
- Tomato sauce – 2 cups
- Basil – 3 tbsp., chopped

Method

1. In a bowl, mix garlic powder and parmesan, and stir.
2. Put flour in a second bowl and the egg in a third.
3. Season chicken with salt and pepper.
4. Dip chicken in flour, then in the egg mix and in panko.
5. Cook chicken pieces in the air fryer at 360F for 3 minutes on each side.
6. Transfer chicken to a baking dish.
7. Add tomato sauce and top with mozzarella.
8. Cook in the air fryer at 375F for 7 minutes.
9. Divide among plates, sprinkle basil on top and serve.

Nutritional Facts Per Serving

- Calories: 304
- Fat: 12g
- Carb: 22g
- Protein: 15g

Mexican Chicken

Prep time: 10 minutes	Cook time: 20 minutes	Servings: 4

Ingredients

- Salsa verde – 16 ounces

- Olive oil – 1 tbsp.
- Salt and black pepper to taste
- Chicken breast – 1 pound, boneless and skinless
- Monetary Jack cheese – 1 ½ cup, grated
- Cilantro – ¼ cup, chopped
- Garlic powder – 1 tsp.

Method

1. Pour salsa verde in a baking dish.
2. Season chicken with garlic powder, salt and pepper, and brush with olive oil. Place over the salsa verde.
3. Place in the air fryer and cook at 380F for 20 minutes.
4. Sprinkle cheese on top and cook for 2 minutes more.
5. Serve.

Nutritional Facts Per Serving

- Calories: 340
- Fat: 18g
- Carb: 32g
- Protein: 18g

Creamy Chicken with Rice

Prep time: 10 minutes	Cook time: 30 minutes	Servings: 4

Ingredients

- Chicken breasts – 1 pound, skinless, boneless and cut into quarters
- White rice – 1 cup, cooked
- Salt and black pepper to taste
- Olive oil – 1 tbsp.
- Garlic – 3 cloves, minced
- Yellow onion – 1, chopped
- White wine – ½ cup
- Heavy cream – ¼ cup
- Chicken stock – 1 cup
- Parsley – ¼ cup, chopped
- Peas – 2 cups, frozen
- Parmesan - 1 ½ cups, grated

Method

1. Season chicken with salt and pepper. Drizzle half of the oil and rub well.
2. Place in the air fryer basket and cook at 360F for 6 minutes.
3. Heat the rest of the oil in a pan. Add garlic, wine, onion, stock, heavy cream, salt and pepper, and stir.
4. Bring to a simmer and cook for 9 minutes.

5. Transfer chicken breasts to a dish and add peas, rice and cream mixture over them. Sprinkle with parsley and parmesan.
6. Place in the air fryer and cook at 420F for 10 minutes.
7. Serve.

Nutritional Facts Per Serving

- Calories: 313
- Fat: 12g
- Carb: 27g
- Protein: 44g

Italian Chicken

Prep time: 10 minutes	Cook time: 16 minutes	Servings: 4

Ingredients

- Chicken thighs – 5
- Olive oil – 1 tbsp.
- Garlic – 2 cloves, minced
- Thyme – 1 tbsp., chopped
- Heavy cream – ½ cup
- Chicken stock – ¾ cup

- Red pepper flakes – 1 tsp., crushed
- Parmesan – ¼ cup, grated
- Sun-dried tomatoes – ½ cup
- Basil – 2 tbsp., chopped
- Salt and black pepper to taste

Method

1. Season chicken with salt and pepper, and rub with half of the oil.
2. Place in the preheated air fryer at 350F and cook for 4 minutes.
3. Meanwhile, heat rest of the oil in a pan and add garlic, thyme, pepper flakes, tomatoes, stock, heavy cream, salt, parmesan and pepper.
4. Bring to a simmer and remove from the heat. Place the mixture in a dish.
5. Add chicken thighs on top and cook in the air fryer at 320F for 12 minutes.
6. Serve with basil sprinkled on top.

Nutritional Facts Per Serving

- Calories: 272
- Fat: 9g
- Carb: 37g

- Protein: 23g

Honey Duck Breasts

| Prep time: 10 minutes | Cook time: 22 minutes | Servings: 2 |

Ingredients

- Smoked duck breast – 1, halved
- Honey – 1 tsp.
- Tomato paste – 1 tsp.
- Mustard – 1 tbsp.
- Apple vinegar – ½ tsp.

Method

1. Mix tomato paste, honey, mustard and vinegar in a bowl. Whisk well.
2. Add duck breast pieces and coat well.
3. Cook in the air fryer at 370F for 15 minutes.
4. Remove the duck breast from the air fryer and add to the honey mixture. Coat again.
5. Cook again at 370F for 6 minutes.
6. Serve.

Nutritional Facts Per Serving

- Calories: 274

- Fat: 11g
- Carb: 22g
- Protein: 13g

Chinese Duck Legs

Prep time: 10 minutes	Cook time: 36 minutes	Servings: 2

Ingredients

- Duck legs – 2
- Dried chilies – 2, chopped
- Olive oil – 1 tbsp.
- Star anise – 2
- Spring onions – 1 bunch, chopped
- Ginger – 4 slices
- Oyster sauce – 1 tbsp.
- Soy sauce – 1 tbsp.
- Sesame oil – 1 tsp.
- Water – 14 ounces
- Rice wine – 1 tbsp.

Method

1. Heat oil in a pan.
2. Add water, soy sauce, oyster sauce, ginger, rice wine, sesame oil, star anise and chili. Stir and cook for 6 minutes.

3. Add spring onions and duck legs, toss to coat and transfer to a pan.
4. Place the pan in the air fryer and cook at 370F for 30 minutes.
5. Serve.

Nutritional Facts Per Serving

- Calories: 300
- Fat: 12g
- Carb: 26g
- Protein: 18g

Duck and Plum Sauce

| Prep time: 10 minutes | Cook time: 32 minutes | Servings: 2 |

Ingredients

- Duck breasts – 2
- Butter – 1 tbsp., melted
- Star anise – 1
- Olive oil – 1 tbsp.
- Shallot – 1, chopped
- Red plumps – 9 ounces, stoned, cut into small wedges

- Sugar – 2 tbsp.
- Red wine – 2 tbsp.
- Beef stock – 1 cup

Method

1. In a pan, heat olive oil over medium heat. Add shallot. Stir-fry for 5 minutes.
2. Add plums and sugar, stir and cook until sugar dissolves.
3. Add wine and stock. Stir and cook for 15 minutes. Remove from heat and keep warm.
4. Score duck breasts, season with salt and pepper. Rub with melted butter, transfer to a heatproof dish. Add plum sauce and star anise.
5. Place in the air fryer and cook at 360F for 12 minutes.
6. Serve.

Nutritional Facts Per Serving

- Calories: 400
- Fat: 25g
- Carb: 29g
- Protein: 44g

Japanese Duck Breasts

Prep time: 10 minutes	Cook time: 20 minutes	Servings: 6

Ingredients

- Duck breasts – 6, boneless
- Soy sauce – 4 tbsp.
- Five-spice powder – 1 ½ tsp.
- Honey – 2 tbsp.
- Salt and black pepper to taste
- Chicken stock – 20 ounces
- Ginger – 4 slices
- Hoisin sauce – 4 tbsp.
- Sesame oil – 1 tsp.

Method

1. In a bowl, mix the five-spice powder with honey, salt, pepper and soy sauce. Whisk, add duck breasts and coat well. Set aside.
2. Heat up the chicken stock, hoisin sauce, ginger and sesame oil in a pan over medium-high heat. Stir well and cook for 3 minutes. Remove from the heat and set aside.
3. Cook duck breasts in the air fryer at 400F for 15 minutes.
4. Divide among plates, drizzle with hoisin and ginger sauce mixture, and serve.

Nutritional Facts Per Serving

- Calories: 336
- Fat: 12g
- Carb: 25g
- Protein: 33g

Duck Breasts with Endives

| Prep time: 10 minutes | Cook time: 25 minutes | Servings: 4 |

Ingredients

- Duck breasts – 2
- Salt and black pepper to taste
- Sugar – 1 tbsp.
- Olive oil – 1 tbsp.
- Endives – 6, julienned
- Cranberries – 2 tbsp.
- White wine – 8 ounces
- Garlic – 1 tbsp., minced
- Heavy cream – 2 tbsp.

Method

1. Score duck breasts and season with salt and pepper.
2. Cook in the air fryer at 350F for 20 minutes. Flip once.

3. Meanwhile, heat up a pan with oil over medium heat. Add endives and sugar. Stir and cook for 2 minutes.
4. Add salt, pepper, wine, garlic, cream and cranberries. Stir fry for 3 minutes.
5. Divide duck breasts among plates. Drizzle with the endives sauce and serve.

Nutritional Facts Per Serving

- Calories: 400
- Fat: 12g
- Carb: 29g
- Protein: 28g

Chicken Salad

| Prep time: 10 minutes | Cook time: 10 minutes | Servings: 4 |

Ingredients

- Chicken breast – 1 pound, boneless, skinless and halved
- Cooking spray
- Salt and black pepper to tray
- Feta cheese – ½ cup, cubed
- Lemon juice – 2 tbsp.
- Mustard – 1 ½ tsp.

- Olive oil – 1 tbsp.
- Red wine vinegar – 1 ½ tsp.
- Anchovies – ½ tsp. minced
- Garlic – ¾ tsp. minced
- Water – 1 tbsp.
- Lettuce leaves – 8 cups, cut into strips
- Parmesan – 4 tbsp., grated

Method

1. Spray chicken breasts with cooking oil. Season with salt and pepper.
2. Place in the air fryer and cook at 370F for 10 minutes. Flip once.
3. Shred the chicken with 2 forks. Put in a salad bowl and mix with lettuce leaves.
4. In a blender, mix feta cheese with lemon juice, olive oil, mustard, vinegar, garlic, anchovies, water and half of the parmesan, and blend very well.
5. Add this over the chicken mixture. Toss and sprinkle with the remaining parmesan then serve.

Nutritional Facts Per Serving

- Calories: 312
- Fat: 6g
- Carb: 22g

- Protein: 26g

Turkey Burgers

| Prep time: 10 minutes | Cook time: 8 minutes | Servings: 4 |

Ingredients

- Turkey meat – 1 pound, ground
- Shallot – 1 minced
- A drizzle of olive oil
- Small jalapeno pepper – 1, minced
- Lime juice – 2 tsp.
- Zest from 1 lime, grated
- Salt and black pepper to taste
- Cumin – 1 tsp., ground
- Sweet paprika – 1 tsp.
- Guacamole for serving

Method

1. In a bowl, combine turkey meat with lime juice, zest, jalapeno, shallot, paprika, cumin, salt and pepper. Mix well.
2. Shape burgers from this mixture and drizzle the oil over them.

3. Cook in the preheated air fryer at 370F for 8 minutes on each side.
4. Divide among plates and serve with guacamole on top.

Nutritional Facts Per Serving

- Calories: 200

- Fat: 12g

- Carb: 0g

- Protein: 12g

Chapter 8: Meat Recipes

Rib Eye Steak

| Prep time: 10 minutes | Cook time: 20 minutes | Servings: 4 |

Ingredients
- Ribeye steak – 2 pounds
- Salt and black pepper to taste
- Olive oil – 1 tbsp.

For the rub
- Sweet paprika – 3 tbsp.
- Onion powder – 2 tbsp.
- Garlic powder – 2 tbsp.
- Brown sugar – 1 tbsp.
- Oregano – 2 tbsp., dried
- Cumin – 1 tbsp., ground
- Rosemary – 1 tbsp., dried

Method

1. Mix cumin, salt, pepper, rosemary, oregano, sugar, garlic powder, onion powder and paprika in a bowl. Stir and rub steak with this mixture.
2. Season steak with salt and pepper, and rub again with the oil.
3. Place in the air fryer and cook at 400F for 20 minutes. Flip once.

4. Slice and serve.

Nutritional Facts Per Serving

- Calories: 320
- Fat: 8g
- Carb: 22g
- Protein: 21g

Chinese Steak and Broccoli

Prep time: 45 minutes	Cook time: 12 minutes	Servings: 4

Ingredients

- Round steak – ¾ pound, cut into strips
- Broccoli florets – 1 pound
- Oyster sauce – 1/3 cup
- Sesame oil – 2 tsp.
- Soy sauce – 1 tsp.
- Sugar – 1 tsp.
- Sherry – 1/3 cup
- Olive oil – 1 tbsp.
- Garlic – 1 clove, minced

Method

1. In a bowl, mix sugar, sherry, soy sauce, oyster sauce and sesame oil. Add beef, toss to coat and marinate for 30 minutes.

2. Transfer to a bowl. Add oil, garlic and broccoli. Toss to coat.
3. Cook at 380F for 12 minutes.
4. Serve.

Nutritional Facts Per Serving
- Calories: 330
- Fat: 12g
- Carb: 23g
- Protein: 23g

Provencal Pork

| Prep time: 10 minutes | Cook time: 15 minutes | Servings: 2 |

Ingredients
- Red onion – 1, sliced
- Yellow bell pepper – 1, cut into strips
- Green bell pepper – 1, cut into strips
- Salt and black pepper to taste
- Provencal herbs – 2 tsp.
- Mustard – ½ tsp.
- Olive oil – 1 tbsp.
- Pork tenderloin – 7 ounces

Method
1. In a dish, mix salt, pepper, onion, green bell pepper, yellow bell pepper, herbs and half the oil, and toss well.

2. Season pork with mustard, salt, pepper and rest of the oil. Toss well and add to veggies.
3. Cook in the air fryer at 370F for 15 minutes.
4. Serve.

Nutritional Facts Per Serving
- Calories: 300
- Fat: 8g
- Carb: 21g
- Protein: 23g

Lamb and Creamy Brussels Sprouts

Prep time: 10 minutes	Cook time: 1 hour and 10 minutes	Servings: 4

Ingredients
- Leg of lamb – 2 pounds, scored
- Olive oil – 2 tbsp.
- Rosemary - 1 tbsp., chopped
- Lemon thyme – 1 tbsp., chopped
- Garlic – 1 clove, minced
- Brussels sprouts – 1 ½ pounds, trimmed
- Butter – 1 tbsp., melted
- Sour cream – ½ cup
- Salt and black pepper to taste

Method

1. Season the leg of lamb with rosemary, thyme, salt and pepper. Brush with oil and place in the air fryer basket.
2. Cook at 300F for 1 hour. Transfer to a plate and keep warm.
3. In a pan, mix Brussels sprouts with sour cream, butter, garlic, salt and pepper. Mix well and cook at 400F for 10 minutes.
4. Divide lamb among plates, add Brussels sprouts on the side and serve.

Nutritional Facts Per Serving

- Calories: 440
- Fat: 23g
- Carb: 2g
- Protein: 49g

Beef Strips with Snow Peas and Mushrooms

Prep time: 10 minutes	Cook time: 22 minutes	Servings: 2

Ingredients

- Beef steaks – 2, cut into strips
- Salt and black pepper to taste
- Snow peas – 7 ounces
- White mushrooms – 8 ounces, halved
- Yellow onion – 1, cut into rings

- Soy sauce – 2 tbsp.
- Olive oil – 1 tsp.

Method
1. In a bowl, mix soy sauce and olive oil, and whisk. Add beef strips and coat.
2. In another bowl, mix mushrooms, onion, snow peas with salt, pepper and the oil. Toss well.
3. Place mushroom mixture in a pan and cook in the air fryer at 350F for 16 minutes.
4. Add beef strips to the pan as well and cook at 400F for 6 minutes more.
5. Serve.

Nutritional Facts Per Serving
- Calories: 235
- Fat: 8g
- Carb: 22g
- Protein: 24g

Garlic Lamb Chops

Prep time: 10 minutes	Cook time: 10 minutes	Servings: 4

Ingredients
- Olive oil – 3 tbsp.
- Lamb chops – 8

- Salt and black pepper to taste
- Garlic – 4 cloves, minced
- Oregano – 1 tbsp., chopped
- Coriander – 1 tbsp., chopped

Method

1. In a bowl, mix oregano with garlic, oil, salt, pepper and lamb chops, and coat well.
2. Cook in the air fryer at 400F for 10 minutes.
3. Serve.

Nutritional Facts Per Serving

- Calories: 231
- Fat: 7g
- Carb: 14g
- Protein: 23g

Crispy Lamb

Prep time: 10 minutes	Cook time: 30 minutes	Servings: 4

Ingredients

- Bread crumbs – 1 tbsp.
- Macadamia nuts – 2 tbsp., toasted and crushed
- Olive oil – 1 tbsp.
- Garlic – 1 clove, minced
- Rack of lamb – 28 ounces
- Salt and black pepper to taste

- o Egg – 1
- o Rosemary – 1 tbsp., chopped

Method

1. Mix oil and garlic in a bowl and stir well.
2. Season lamb with salt and pepper, and brush with oil.
3. In another bowl, mix nuts with rosemary and breadcrumbs.
4. Put the egg in a separate bowl and whisk well.
5. Dip lamb in egg, then in macadamia mix.
6. Place them in air fryer basket. Cook at 360F for 25 minutes.
7. Increase heat to 400F and cook for 5 minutes more.
8. Serve.

Nutritional Facts Per Serving

- o Calories: 230
- o Fat: 2g
- o Carb: 10g
- o Protein: 12g

Indian Pork

Prep time: 35 minutes	Cook time: 10 minutes	Servings: 4

Ingredients

- o Ginger powder – 1 tsp.
- o Chili paste – 2 tsp.

- Garlic cloves – 2, minced
- Pork chops – 14 ounces, cubed
- Shallot – 1, chopped
- Coriander – 1 tsp. ground
- Coconut milk – 7 ounces
- Olive oil – 2 tbsp.
- Peanuts – 3 ounces, ground
- Soy sauce – 3 tbsp.
- Salt and black pepper to taste

Method

1. In a bowl, mix ginger powder with half the oil, half of the soy sauce, half of the garlic and 1 tsp. chili paste. Whisk and add meat. Coat and marinate for 10 minutes.
2. Cook the meat at 400F in the air fryer for 12 minutes.
3. Meanwhile, heat up the pan with the rest of the oil and add the peanuts, coconut milk, coriander, shallot, the rest of the garlic, chili paste, and soy sauce. Stir-fry for 5 minutes.
4. Divide pork among plates, spread coconut mixture on top and serve.

Nutritional Facts Per Serving

- Calories: 423
- Fat: 11g
- Carb: 42g
- Protein: 18g

Beef Fillets with Garlic Mayo

| Prep time: 10 minutes | Cook time: 40 minutes | Servings: 8 |

Ingredients
- Mayonnaise – 1 cup
- Sour cream – 1/3 cup
- Garlic – 3 cloves, minced
- Beef fillet – 3 pounds
- Chives – 2 tbsp., chopped
- Mustard – 2 tbsp.
- Tarragon – ¼ cup, chopped
- Salt and black pepper to taste

Method
1. Season beef with salt and pepper and place in the air fryer.
2. Cook at 370F for 20 minutes. Transfer to a plate and set aside.
3. In a bowl, mix garlic with salt, pepper, mayo, chives and sour cream. Whisk and set aside.
4. In another bowl, mix mustard with tarragon and Dijon mustard. Whisk and add beef. Mix well.
5. Return beef to the air fryer and cook at 350F for 20 minutes more.
6. Divide beef among plates, spread garlic mayo on top and serve.

Nutritional Facts Per Serving
- Calories: 400
- Fat: 12g
- Carb: 27g
- Protein: 19g

Mustard Marinated Beef

Prep time: 10 minutes	Cook time: 45 minutes	Servings: 6

Ingredients
- Bacon strips – 6
- Butter – 2 tbsp.
- Garlic – 3 cloves, minced
- Salt and black pepper to taste
- Horseradish – 1 tbsp.
- Mustard – 1 tbsp.
- Beef roast – 3 pounds
- Beef stock – 1 ¾ cup
- Red wine – ¾ cup

Method
1. In a bowl, mix butter with horseradish, salt, pepper, garlic and mustard. Whisk and rub the beef with this mixture.
2. Arrange bacon strips on a cutting board. Place beef on top and fold bacon around beef.

3. Place in the air fryer basket and cook at 400F for 15 minutes and transfer to a pan.
4. Add stock and wine to the beef. Place the pan in the air fryer and cook at 360F for 30 minutes.
5. Carve beef, divide among plates and serve.

Nutritional Facts Per Serving
- Calories: 500
- Fat: 9g
- Carb: 29g
- Protein: 36g

Creamy Pork

Prep time: 10 minutes	Cook time: 22 minutes	Servings: 6

Ingredients
- Pork meat – 2 pounds, boneless and cubed
- Yellow onions – 2, chopped
- Olive oil – 1 tbsp.
- Garlic – 1 clove, minced
- Chicken stock – 3 cups
- Sweet paprika – 2 tbsp.
- Salt and black pepper to taste
- White flour – 2 tbsp.
- Sour cream – 1 ½ cups
- Dill – 2 tbsp., chopped

Method
1. In a pan, mix pork with oil, salt and pepper. .

2. Place in the air fryer and cook at 360F for 7 minutes.
3. Add the sour cream, dill, flour, paprika, stock, garlic and onion. Mix well.
4. Cook at 370F for 15 minutes more.
5. Serve.

Nutritional Facts Per Serving
- Calories: 300
- Fat: 4g
- Carb: 26g
- Protein: 34g

Marinated Pork Chops and Onions

| Prep time: 24 hours | Cook time: 25 minutes | Servings: 6 |

Ingredients
- Pork chops – 2
- Olive oil – ¼ cup
- Yellow onions – 2, sliced
- Garlic cloves – 2, minced
- Mustard – 2 tsp.
- Sweet paprika – 1 tsp.
- Salt and black pepper to taste
- Oregano – ½ tsp. dried
- Thyme – ½ tsp. dried
- A pinch of cayenne pepper

Method

1. In a bowl, mix oil with cayenne, thyme, oregano, black pepper, paprika, mustard and garlic. Whisk well.
2. Combine onions with meat and mustard mixture. Toss to coat, cover and marinate in the refrigerator for 1 day.
3. Transfer meat and onion mixture to a pan and cook in the air fryer at 360F for 25 minutes.
4. Serve.

Nutritional Facts Per Serving

- Calories: 384
- Fat: 4g
- Carb: 17g
- Protein: 25g

Simple Braised Pork

Prep time: 40 minutes	Cook time: 40 minutes	Servings: 4

Ingredients

- Pork loin roast – 2 pounds, boneless and cubed
- Butter – 4 tbsp., melted
- Salt and black pepper to taste
- Chicken stock – 2 cups
- Dry white wine – ½ cup
- Garlic – 2 cloves, minced
- Thyme – 1 tsp., chopped
- Thyme spring – 1

- Bay leaf – 1
- Yellow onion – ½, chopped
- White flour – 2 tbsp.
- Red grapes – ½ pound

Method
1. Season pork cubes with salt and pepper. Rub with 2 tbsp. melted butter and put in the air fryer.
2. Cook at 370F for 8 minutes.
3. Meanwhile, heat up a pan with 2 tbsp. butter over medium heat. Add onion and garlic, and stir-fry for 2 minutes.
4. Add bay leaf, flour, thyme, salt, pepper, stock and wine. Mix well. Bring to a simmer then remove from the heat.
5. Add grapes and pork cubes. Cook in the air fryer at 360F for 30 minutes.
6. Serve.

Nutritional Facts Per Serving
- Calories: 320
- Fat: 4g
- Carb: 29g
- Protein: 38g

Pork with Couscous

| Prep time: 10 minutes | Cook time: 35 minutes | Servings: 6 |

Ingredients

- Pork loin – 2 ½ pounds, boneless and trimmed
- Chicken stock – ¾ cup
- Olive oil – 2 tbsp.
- Sweet paprika – ½ tbsp.
- Dried sage – 2 ¼ tsp.
- Garlic powder – ½ tsp.
- Dried rosemary – ¼ tsp.
- Dried marjoram – ¼ tsp.
- Dried basil – 1 tsp.
- Dried oregano – 1 tsp.
- Salt and black pepper to taste
- Couscous – 2 cups, cooked

Method

1. In a bowl, mix oil with stock, salt, pepper, oregano, marjoram, thyme, rosemary, sage, garlic powder and paprika. Whisk well and add pork loin. Mix and marinate for 1 hour.
2. Cook in the air fryer at 370F for 35 minutes.
3. Divide among plates and serve with couscous on the side.

Nutritional Facts Per Serving

- Calories: 310
- Fat: 4g

- Carb: 37g
- Protein: 34g

Beef Brisket and Onion Sauce

| Prep time: 10 minutes | Cook time: 2 hours | Servings: 6 |

Ingredients
- Yellow onion – 1 pound, chopped
- Beef brisket – 4 pounds
- Carrot – 1 pound, chopped
- Tea bags – 8
- Celery – ½ pound, chopped
- Salt and black pepper to taste
- Water – 4 cups

Sauce
- Canned tomatoes – 16 ounces, chopped
- Celery – ½ pound, chopped
- Garlic – 1 ounce, minced
- Vegetable oil – 4 ounces
- Sweet onion – 1 pound, chopped
- Brown sugar – 1 cup
- Tea bags – 8
- White vinegar – 1 cup

Method

1. Put 4 cups water in a dish. Add ½ pound celery, 1 pound carrot, 1 pound onion, salt and pepper. Stir and bring to a simmer over medium heat.
2. Add 8 tea bags and beef brisket. Stir, transfer to the air fryer basket and cook at 300F for 1 hour and 30 minutes.
3. Meanwhile, heat up a pan with vegetable oil over medium-high heat. Add 1 pound onion. Stir fry for 10 minutes.
4. Add 8 tea bags, salt, pepper, vinegar, sugar, tomatoes, garlic and ½ pound celery. Stir and bring to a simmer. Cook for 10 minutes and discard tea bags.
5. Slice the beef brisket. Drizzle with onion sauce and serve.

Nutritional Facts Per Serving

- Calories: 400
- Fat: 12g
- Carb: 38g
- Protein: 34g

Beef and Green Onions Marinade

Prep time: 10 minutes	Cook time: 20 minutes	Servings: 4

Ingredients

- Green onion – 1 cup, chopped
- Soy sauce – 1 cup

- Water – ½ cup
- Brown sugar – ¼ cup
- Sesame seeds – ¼ cup
- Garlic – 5 cloves, minced
- Black pepper – 1 tsp.
- Lean beef – 1 pound

Method
1. In a bowl, mix the onion with water, soy sauce, garlic, sugar, sesame seeds and pepper. Whisk and add beef. Marinate for 10 minutes.
2. Drain beef. Cook in the preheated air fryer at 390F for 20 minutes.
3. Serve.

Nutritional Facts Per Serving
- Calories: 329
- Fat: 8g
- Carb: 26g
- Protein: 22g

Marinated Lamb and Veggies

Prep time: 10 minutes	Cook time: 30 minutes	Servings: 4

Ingredients
- Carrot – 1, chopped
- Onion – 1, sliced

- Olive oil – ½ tbsp.
- Bean sprouts – 3 ounces
- Lamb loin – 8 ounces, sliced

For the marinade
- Garlic – 1 clove, minced
- Apple – ½, grated
- Salt and black pepper to taste
- Small yellow onion – 1, grated
- Grated ginger – 1 tbsp.
- Soy sauce – 5 tbsp.
- Sugar – 1 tbsp.
- Orange juice – 2 tbsp.

Method
1. In a bowl, mix 1 grated onion with black pepper, sugar, orange juice, soy sauce, 1 tbsp. ginger, garlic and apple. Whisk and add the lamb. Coat and marinate for 10 minutes.
2. Heat olive oil in a pan over medium-high heat. Add 1 sliced onion, bean sprouts and carrot. Stir fry for 3 minutes.
3. Add lamb and the marinade.
4. Place the pan in the preheated air fryer and cook at 360F for 25 minutes.
5. Serve.

Nutritional Facts Per Serving
- Calories: 265
- Fat: 3g
- Carb: 18g
- Protein: 22g

Creamy Lamb

| Prep time: 1 day | Cook time: 1 hour | Servings: 8 |

Ingredients
- Leg of lamb – 5 pounds
- Low-fat buttermilk – 2 cups
- Mustard – 2 tbsp.
- Butter – ½ cup
- Basil – 2 tbsp., chopped
- Tomato paste – 2 tbsp.
- Garlic – 2 cloves, minced
- Salt and black pepper to taste
- White wine – 1 cup
- Cornstarch – 1 tbsp. mixed with 1 tbsp. water
- Sour cream – ½ cup

Method
1. Place lamb roast in a dish. Add buttermilk and toss to coat. Cover and marinate in the refrigerator for 24 hours.
2. Pat dry lamb and put in a pan that fits in the air fryer basket.

3. In a bowl, mix butter with garlic, salt, pepper, rosemary, basil, mustard and tomato paste. Whisk well and spread over the lamb.
4. Place in the air fryer and cook at 300F for 1 hour.
5. Slice lamb, divide among plates.
6. Heat up cooking juices from the pan on the stove.
7. Add sour cream, salt, pepper, wine and cornstarch mix.
8. Remove from heat and drizzle lamb with this sauce.
9. Serve.

Nutritional Facts Per Serving
- Calories: 287
- Fat: 4g
- Carb: 19g
- Protein: 25g

Lamb Shanks

Prep time: 10 minutes	Cook time: 45 minutes	Servings: 4

Ingredients
- Lamb shanks – 4
- Yellow onion – 1, chopped
- Olive oil – 1 tbsp.
- Coriander seeds – 4 tsp., crushed
- White flour – 2 tbsp.

- Bay leaves – 4
- Honey – 2 tsp.
- Dry sherry – 5 ounces
- Chicken stock – 2 ½ cups
- Salt and pepper to taste

Method

1. Season the lamb shanks with salt and pepper. Rub with half of the oil and cook in the air fryer at 360F for 10 minutes.
2. Heat up a pan that fits in the air fryer with the rest of the oil over medium-high heat. Add onion and coriander. Stir and cook for 5 minutes.
3. Add salt, pepper, bay leaves, honey, stock, sherry and flour. Stir, bring to a simmer, and add the lamb. Mix well.
4. Cook in the air fryer at 360F for 30 minutes.
5. Serve.

Nutritional Facts Per Serving

- Calories: 283
- Fat: 4g
- Carb: 17g
- Protein: 26g

Lamb Roast and Potatoes

| Prep time: 10 minutes | Cook time: 45 minutes | Servings: 6 |

Ingredients
- Lamb roast – 4 pounds
- Rosemary – 1 spring
- Garlic – 3 cloves, minced
- Potatoes – 6, halved
- Lamb stock – ½ cup
- Bay leaves – 4
- Salt and pepper to taste

Method
1. Put potatoes in a dish. Add salt, pepper, rosemary spring, garlic, bay leaves, stock and lamb. Mix and place in the air fryer.
2. Cook at 360F for 45 minutes.
3. Slice lamb, divide among plates, and serve with potatoes and cooking juices.

Nutritional Facts Per Serving
- Calories: 273
- Fat: 4g
- Carb: 25g
- Protein: 29g

Chapter 9: Vegetable Recipes

Spinach Pie

| Prep time: 10 minutes | Cook time: 15 minutes | Servings: 4 |

Ingredients
- Flour – 7 ounces
- Butter – 2 tbsp.
- Spinach – 7 ounces
- Olive oil – 1 tbsp.
- Eggs – 2
- Milk – 2 tbsp.
- Cottage cheese – 3 ounces
- Salt and black pepper to taste
- Yellow onion – 1, chopped

Method

1. In a food processor, mix flour with butter, milk, 1 egg, salt and pepper. Blend well and transfer to a bowl. Knead, cover and leave for 10 minutes.
2. Heat the oil in a pan over medium-high heat. Add spinach and onion. Stir-fry for 2 minutes.
3. Add the remaining egg, cottage cheese, salt and pepper. Mix well and remove from the heat.
4. Divide dough into 4 pieces. Roll each piece and place on the bottom of a ramekin. Add spinach filling over

dough, place ramekins in the air fryer basket and cook at 360F for 15 minutes.
5. Serve.

Nutritional Facts Per Serving

- Calories: 250
- Fat: 12g
- Carb: 23g
- Protein: 12g

Balsamic Artichokes

| Prep time: 10 minutes | Cook time: 7 minutes | Servings: 4 |

Ingredients

- Big artichokes – 4, trimmed
- Salt and black pepper to taste
- Lemon juice – 2 tbsp.
- Extra-virgin olive oil – ¼ cup
- Balsamic vinegar – 2 tsp.
- Oregano – 1 tsp., dried
- Garlic – 2 cloves, minced

Method

1. Season artichokes with salt and pepper. Rub with half of the lemon juice and half of the oil. Cook in the air fryer at 360F for 7 minutes.

2. Meanwhile, in a bowl, combine the remaining oil and lemon juice with vinegar, salt, pepper, garlic and oregano. Mix well.
3. Arrange artichokes on a platter. Drizzle the balsamic vinaigrette over them and serve.

Nutritional Facts Per Serving
- Calories: 200
- Fat: 3g
- Carb: 12g
- Protein: 4g

Beet Salad and Parsley Dressing

Prep time: 10 minutes	Cook time: 14 minutes	Servings: 4

Ingredients
- Beets – 4
- Balsamic vinegar – 2 tbsp.
- Parsley – 1 bunch, chopped
- Salt and black pepper to taste
- Extra-virgin olive oil – 1 tbsp.
- Garlic – 1 clove, chopped
- Capers – 2 tbsp.

Method
1. Put beets in the air fryer and cook at 360F for 14 minutes.

2. Meanwhile, in a bowl, combine garlic, parsley, olive oil, salt, pepper and capers, and mix well.
3. Remove the beets then cool. Peel and slice them.
4. Add vinegar, drizzle the parsley dressing over and serve.

Nutritional Facts Per Serving
- Calories: 70
- Fat: 2g
- Carb: 6g
- Protein: 4g

Broccoli Salad

| Prep time: 10 minutes | Cook time: 8 minutes | Servings: 4 |

Ingredients
- Broccoli – 1 head, florets separated
- Peanut oil – 1 tbsp.
- Garlic – 6 cloves, minced
- Chinese rice wine vinegar – 1 tbsp.
- Salt and black pepper to taste

Method
1. In a bowl, mix broccoli with half of the oil, salt and pepper, and toss.
2. Cook in the air fryer at 350F for 8 minutes. Shake once.

3. Transfer broccoli to a bowl. Add the rest of the peanut oil, rice vinegar and garlic, and toss well.
4. Serve.

Nutritional Facts Per Serving
- Calories: 121
- Fat: 3g
- Carb: 4g
- Protein: 4g

Brussels Sprouts and Tomatoes Mix

| Prep time: 5 minutes | Cook time: 10 minutes | Servings: 4 |

Ingredients
- Brussels sprouts – 1 pound, trimmed
- Salt and black pepper to taste
- Cherry tomatoes – 6, halved
- Green onions – ¼ cup, chopped
- Olive oil – 1 tbsp.

Method
1. Season Brussels sprouts with salt and pepper.
2. Cook in the air fryer at 350F for 10 minutes.
3. Transfer to a bowl. Add olive oil, green onions, cherry tomatoes, salt and pepper. Toss and serve.

Nutritional Facts Per Serving
- Calories: 121
- Fat: 4g
- Carb: 11g

- Protein: 4g

Spicy Cabbage

| Prep time: 10 minutes | Cook time: 8 minutes | Servings: 4 |

Ingredients
- Cabbage – 1, cut into 8 wedges
- Sesame seed oil – 1 tbsp.
- Carrot – 1, grated
- Apple cider vinegar – ¼ cup
- Apple juice – ¼ cup
- Cayenne pepper – ½ tsp.
- Red pepper flakes – 1 tsp., crushed

Method

1. In a pan, combine cabbage with pepper flakes, cayenne, apple juice, vinegar, carrot and oil. Toss to mix.
2. Place the pan in the preheated air fryer and cook at 350F for 8 minutes.
3. Arrange cabbage mixture on plates and serve.

Nutritional Facts Per Serving

- Calories: 100
- Fat: 4g
- Carb: 11g
- Protein: 7g

Sweet Baby Carrots Dish

| Prep time: 10 minutes | Cook time: 10 minutes | Servings: 4 |

Ingredients
- Baby carrots – 2 cups
- Salt and black pepper to taste
- Brown sugar – 1 tbsp.
- Butter – ½ tbsp., melted

Method

1. In a dish, mix baby carrots with sugar, butter, salt and pepper.
2. Place the dish in the air fryer and cook at 350F for 10 minutes.
3. Serve.

Nutritional Facts Per Serving

- Calories: 100
- Fat: 2g
- Carb: 7g
- Protein: 4g

Collard Greens Mix

| Prep time: 10 minutes | Cook time: 10 minutes | Servings: 4 |

Ingredients
- Collard greens – 1 bunch, trimmed

- Olive oil – 2 tbsp.
- Tomato paste – 2 tbsp.
- Yellow onion – 1, chopped
- Garlic – 3 cloves, minced
- Salt and black pepper to taste
- Balsamic vinegar – 1 tbsp.
- Sugar – 1 tsp.

Method

1. In a bowl, mix tomato puree, onion, vinegar, garlic and oil. Whisk.
2. Add sugar, salt, pepper and collard greens. Mix.
3. Place the bowl in the air fryer and cook at 320F for 10 minutes.
4. Serve.

Nutritional Facts Per Serving

- Calories: 121
- Fat: 3g
- Carb: 7g
- Protein: 3g

Herbed Eggplant and Zucchini Mix

| Prep time: 10 minutes | Cook time: 8 minutes | Servings: 4 |

Ingredients
- Eggplant – 1, cubed
- Zucchinis – 3, roughly cubed

- Lemon juice – 2 tbsp.
- Salt and black pepper to taste
- Thyme – 1 tsp., dried
- Oregano – 1 tsp., dried
- Olive oil – 3 tbsp.

Method

1. Put eggplant in a dish. Add olive oil, oregano, thyme, salt, pepper, lemon juice and zucchinis. Toss to mix.
2. Place the dish in the air fryer and at 360F for 8 minutes.
3. Serve.

Nutritional Facts Per Serving

- Calories: 152
- Fat: 5g
- Carb: 19g
- Protein: 5g

Flavored Fennel

| Prep time: 10 minutes | Cook time: 8 minutes | Servings: 4 |

Ingredients

- Fennel bulbs – 2, cut into quarters
- Olive oil – 3 tbsp.
- Salt and black pepper to taste
- Garlic – 1 clove, minced
- Red chili pepper – 1, chopped

- Veggie stock – ¾ cup
- Juice of a ½ lemon
- White wine – ¼ cup
- Parmesan – ¼ cup, grated

Method

1. Heat oil in a pan over medium-high heat. Add garlic and chili pepper. Stir-fry for 2 minutes.
2. Add parmesan, lemon juice, wine, stock, salt, pepper and fennel. Toss to coat.
3. Place the pan in the air fryer and cook at 350F for 6 minutes.
4. Serve.

Nutritional Facts Per Serving

- Calories: 100
- Fat: 4g
- Carb: 4g
- Protein: 4g

Okra and Corn Salad

Prep time: 10 minutes	Cook time: 12 minutes	Servings: 6

Ingredients
- Okra – 1 pound, trimmed
- Scallions – 6, chopped
- Green bell peppers – 3, chopped

- o   Salt and black pepper to taste
- o   Olive oil – 2 tbsp.
- o   Sugar – 1 tsp.
- o   Canned tomatoes – 28 ounces, chopped
- o   Corn – 1 cup

Method
1. Heat oil in a pan over medium-high heat. Add bell peppers and scallions, stir and cook for 5 minutes.
2. Add corn, tomatoes, sugar, salt, pepper and okra. Mix.
3. Place the pan in the air fryer and cook at 360F for 7 minutes.
4. Serve.

Nutritional Facts Per Serving
- o   Calories: 152
- o   Fat: 4g
- o   Carb: 18g
- o   Protein: 4g

Air Fried Leeks

| Prep time: 10 minutes | Cook time: 7 minutes | Servings: 4 |

Ingredients
- o   Leeks – 4, washed, ends cut and halved
- o   Salt and black pepper to taste
- o   Butter – 1 tbsp., melted
- o   Lemon juice – 1 tbsp.

Method
1. Rub leeks with melted butter and season with salt and pepper.
2. Place in the air fryer and cook at 350F for 7 minutes.
3. Arrange on a platter. Drizzle with lemon juice and serve.

Nutritional Facts Per Serving
- Calories: 100
- Fat: 4g
- Carb: 6g
- Protein: 2g

Crispy Potatoes and Parsley

Prep time: 10 minutes	Cook time: 10 minutes	Servings: 4

Ingredients
- Gold potatoes – 1 pound, cut into wedges
- Salt and black pepper to taste
- Olive oil – 2 tbsp.
- Juice from a ½ lemon
- Parsley leaves – ¼ cup, chopped

Method
1. Rub potatoes with olive oil, lemon juice, salt and pepper.
2. Put them in the air fryer and cook at 350F for 10 minutes.

3. Divide among plates, sprinkle parsley on top and serve.

Nutritional Facts Per Serving
- Calories: 152
- Fat: 3g
- Carb: 17g
- Protein: 4g

Turnips Salad

| Prep time: 10 minutes | Cook time: 12 minutes | Servings: 4 |

Ingredients
- Turnips – 20 ounces, peeled and chopped
- Garlic – 1 tsp., minced
- Ginger – 1 tsp., grated
- Yellow onion – 2, chopped
- Tomatoes – 2, chopped
- Cumin – 1 tsp., ground
- Coriander – 1 tsp., ground
- Green chilies – 2, chopped
- Turmeric powder – ½ tsp.
- Butter – 2 tbsp.
- Salt and black pepper to taste
- Chopped coriander leaves – 1 handful

Method
1. Melt the butter in a pan. Add ginger, garlic and green chilies. Stir-fry for 1 minute.
2. Add turnips, ground coriander, cumin, turmeric, tomatoes, salt, pepper and onions. Stir to mix.
3. Place in the air fryer and cook at 350F for 10 minutes.
4. Sprinkle with fresh coriander and serve.

Nutritional Facts Per Serving
- Calories: 100
- Fat: 3g
- Carb: 12g
- Protein: 4g

Chapter 10: Dessert Recipes

Banana Cake

Prep time: 10 minutes	Cook time: 30 minutes	Servings: 4

Ingredients
- Soft butter – 1 tbsp.
- Egg – 1
- Brown sugar – 1/3 cup
- Honey – 2 tbsp.
- Banana – 1, peeled and mashed
- White flour – 1 cup
- Baking powder – 1 tsp.
- Cinnamon powder – ½ tsp.
- Cooking spray

Method
1. Spray a cake pan with cooking spray and set aside.
2. In a bowl, mix flour, baking powder, cinnamon, egg, honey, banana, sugar and butter. Whisk.
3. Pour the batter into the greased cake pan and cook in the air fryer at 350F for 30 minutes.
4. Cool, slice and serve.

Nutritional Facts Per Serving
- Calories: 232
- Fat: 4g

- Carb: 34g
- Protein: 4g

Simple Cheesecake

| Prep time: 10 minutes | Cook time: 15 minutes | Servings: 15 |

Ingredients
- Cream cheese – 1 pound
- Vanilla extract – ½ tsp.
- Eggs – 2
- Sugar – 4 tbsp.
- Graham crackers – 1 cup, crumbled
- Butter – 2 tbsp.

Method
1. Mix crackers with the butter in a bowl.
2. Press crackers mixture on the bottom of a lined cake pan.
3. Place in the air fryer and cook at 350F for 4 minutes.
4. Meanwhile, in a bowl, mix eggs, cream cheese, sugar and vanilla, and whisk well.
5. Spread filling over crackers crust and cook in the air fryer at 310F for 15 minutes.
6. Cool and keep in the refrigerator for 3 hours.
7. Slice and serve.

Nutritional Facts Per Serving
- Calories: 245

- o Fat: 12g
- o Carb: 20g
- o Protein: 3g

Bread Pudding

| Prep time: 10 minutes | Cook time: 1 hour | Servings: 4 |

Ingredients
- o Glazed doughnuts – 6, crumbled
- o Cherries – 1 cup
- o Egg – 4 yolks
- o Whipping cream – 1 ½ cups
- o Raisins – ½ cup
- o Sugar – ¼ cup
- o Chocolate chips – ½ cup

Method

1. In a bowl, mix cherries with egg yolks and whipping cream, and stir well.
2. In another bowl, mix doughnuts, chocolate chips, sugar and raisins.
3. Combine 2 mixtures and transfer everything to a greased pan that fits in your air fryer and cook at 310F for 1 hour.
4. Chill pudding before cutting then serve.

Nutritional Facts Per Serving

- o Calories: 302
- o Fat: 8g

- Carb: 23g
- Protein: 10g

Cinnamon Rolls and Cream Cheese Dip

| Prep time: 2 hours | Cook time: 15 minutes | Servings: 8 |

Ingredients
- Bread dough – 1 pound
- Brown sugar – ¾ cup
- Cinnamon – 1 ½ tbsp., ground
- Butter – ¼ cup, melted

For the cream cheese dip
- Butter – 2 tbsp.
- Cream cheese – 4 ounces
- Sugar – 1 ¼ cups
- Vanilla – ½ tsp.

Method
1. Roll dough on a floured working surface, shape a rectangle and brush with ¼ cup butter.
2. Mix sugar and cinnamon in a bowl. Sprinkle this over dough. Roll dough into a log. Seal well and cut into 8 pieces.
3. Leave rolls to rise for 2 hours. Place them in the air fryer basket.
4. Cook at 350F for 5 minutes. Then flip and cook for 4 minutes more.
5. Transfer to a platter.

6. In a bowl, mix butter, cream cheese, sugar and vanilla. Whisk well.
7. Serve cinnamon rolls with this cream cheese dip.

Nutritional Facts Per Serving
- Calories: 200
- Fat: 1g
- Carb: 5g
- Protein: 6g

Pumpkin Pie

Prep time: 10 minutes	Cook time: 15 minutes	Servings: 9

Ingredients
- Sugar – 1 tbsp.
- Flour – 2 tbsp.
- Butter – 1 tbsp.
- Water – 2 tbsp.

For the pumpkin pie filling
- Pumpkin flesh – 3.5 ounces, chopped
- Mixed spice – 1 tsp.
- Nutmeg – 1 tsp.
- Water – 3 ounces
- Egg – 1, whisked
- Sugar – 1 tbsp.

Method

1. Put 3 ounces water in a pot. Bring to a boil and add pumpkin, 1 tbsp. sugar, egg, spice and nutmeg. Stir and boil for 20 minutes.
2. Remove from the heat and blend with a hand mixer.
3. In a bowl, mix butter, flour, 2 tbsp. water and 1 tbsp. sugar. Knead the dough well.
4. Grease a pie pan with butter. Press dough into the pan. Fill with pumpkin pie filling.
5. Place in the air fryer basket and cook at 360F for 15 minutes.
6. Serve.

Nutritional Facts Per Serving

- Calories: 200
- Fat: 5g
- Carb: 5g
- Protein: 6g

Strawberry Donuts

Prep time: 10 minutes	Cook time: 15 minutes	Servings: 4

Ingredients

- Flour – 8 ounces
- Brown sugar – 1 tbsp.
- White sugar – 1 tbsp.
- Egg – 1
- Butter – 2 ½ tbsp.
- Whole milk – 4 ounces

- Baking powder – 1 tsp.

For the strawberry icing
- Butter – 2 tbsp.
- Icing sugar – 3.5 ounces
- Pink coloring – ½ tsp.
- Strawberries – ¼ cup, chopped
- Whipped cream – 1 tbsp.

Method

1. In a bowl, mix flour, 1 tbsp. white sugar, 1 tbsp. brown sugar and butter, and stir.
2. In another bowl, mix the egg with 1 ½ tbsp. butter and milk, and stir well.
3. Combine the 2 mixtures, stir, then shape donuts from this mix. Place them in the air fryer basket and cook at 360F for 15 minutes.
4. Mix strawberry puree, whipped cream, food coloring, icing sugar and 1 tbsp. butter, and whisk well.
5. Arrange donuts on a platter and serve with strawberry icing on top.

Nutritional Facts Per Serving
- Calories: 250
- Fat: 12g
- Carb: 32g
- Protein: 4g

Cocoa Cake

| Prep time: 10 minutes | Cook time: 17 minutes | Servings: 6 |

Ingredients
- Butter – 3.5 ounces, melted
- Eggs – 3
- Sugar – 3 ounces
- Cocoa powder – 1 tsp.
- Flour – 3 ounces
- Lemon juice – ½ tsp.

Method
1. In a bowl, mix cocoa powder with 1 tbsp. butter and whisk.
2. In another bowl, mix the rest of the butter with lemon juice, flour, eggs and sugar. Whisk well and pour half into a cake pan.
3. Add half of the cocoa mix, spread, add the rest of the butter layer and top with the rest of the cocoa.
4. Cook in the air fryer at 360F for 17 minutes.
5. Cool, slice and serve.

Nutritional Facts Per Serving
- Calories: 340
- Fat: 11g
- Carb: 25g
- Protein: 5g

Chocolate Cake

| Prep time: 10 minutes | Cook time: 30 minutes | Servings: 12 |

Ingredients
- White flour – ¾ cup
- Whole wheat flour – ¾ cup
- Baking soda – 1 tsp.
- Pumpkin pie spice – ¾ tsp.
- Sugar – ¾ cup
- Banana – 1, mashed
- Baking powder – ½ tsp.
- Canola oil – 2 tbsp.
- Greek yogurt – ½ cup
- Canned pumpkin puree – 8 ounces
- Cooking spray
- Egg – 1
- Vanilla extract – ½ tsp.
- Chocolate chips – 2/3 cup

Method

1. In a bowl, mix whole wheat flour, white flour, salt, baking soda, baking powder and pumpkin spice, and stir.
2. In another bowl, combine egg, vanilla, pumpkin puree, yogurt, banana, oil and sugar. Mix with a mixer.
3. Combine the 2 mixtures and add chocolate chips. Pour this into a greased Bundit pan.

4. Place in the air fryer and cook at 330F for 30 minutes.
5. Cool, slice and serve.

Nutritional Facts Per Serving
- Calories: 232
- Fat: 7g
- Carb: 29g
- Protein: 4g

Apple Bread

Prep time: 10 minutes	Cook time: 40 minutes	Servings: 6

Ingredients
- Apples – 3, cored and cubed
- Sugar – 1 cup
- Vanilla – 1 tbsp.
- Eggs – 2
- Apple pie spice – 1 tbsp.
- White flour – 2 cups
- Baking powder – 1 tbsp.
- Butter – 1 stick
- Water – 1 cup

Method
1. In a bowl, mix 1 stick butter, egg, apple pie spice and sugar. Stir with a mixer.

2. Add apples and stir well.
3. In another bowl, mix flour and baking powder.
4. Combine the 2 mixtures. Stir and pour into a springform pan.
5. Put springform pan in the air fryer and cook at 320F for 40 minutes.
6. Slice and serve.

Nutritional Facts Per Serving
- Calories: 192
- Fat: 6g
- Carb: 14g
- Protein: 7g

Mini Lava Cakes

Prep time: 10 minutes	Cook time: 20 minutes	Servings: 3

Ingredients
- Egg – 1
- Sugar – 4 tbsp.
- Olive oil – 2 tbsp.
- Milk – 4 tbsp.
- Flour – 4 tbsp.
- Cocoa powder – 1 tbsp.
- Baking powder – ½ tsp.
- Orange zest – ½ tsp.

Method

1. In a bowl, combine oil, sugar, milk, egg, flour, salt, cocoa powder, baking powder and orange zest. Mix well and pour into greased ramekins.
2. Add ramekins to the air fryer and cook at 320F for 20 minutes.
3. Serve.

Nutritional Facts Per Serving

- Calories: 201
- Fat: 7g
- Carb: 23g
- Protein: 4g

Carrot Cake

Prep time: 10 minutes	Cook time: 45 minutes	Servings: 6

Ingredients

- Flour – 5 ounces
- Baking powder – ¾ tsp.
- Baking soda – ½ tsp.
- Cinnamon powder – ½ tsp.
- Allspice – ½ tsp.
- Nutmeg – ¼ tsp. ground
- Egg – 1
- Yogurt – 3 tbsp.
- Sugar – ½ cup

- Pineapple juice – ¼ cup
- Sunflower oil – 4 tbsp.
- Carrots – 1/3 cup, grated
- Pecans – 1/3 cup, toasted and chopped
- Coconut flakes – 1/3 cup, shredded
- Cooking spray

Method
1. In a bowl, combine flour, nutmeg, cinnamon, allspice, salt, baking soda and powder, and mix.
2. In another bowl, mix the egg with coconut flakes, pecans, carrots, oil, pineapple juice, sugar and yogurt.
3. Combine the two mixtures and mix well. Pour this into a greased springform pan.
4. Place the pan in the air fryer and cook at 320F for 45 minutes.
5. Cool, slice and serve.

Nutritional Facts Per Serving
- Calories: 200
- Fat: 6g
- Carb: 22g
- Protein: 4g

Ginger Cheesecake

| Prep time: 2 hours and 10 minutes | Cook time: 20 minutes | Servings: 6 |

Ingredients
- Butter – 2 tsp., melted
- Ginger cookies – ½ cup, crumbled
- Cream cheese – 16 ounces, soft
- Eggs – 2
- Sugar – ½ cup
- Rum – 1 tsp.
- Vanilla extract – ½ tsp.
- Nutmeg – ½ tsp., ground

Method

1. Grease a pan with butter and spread cookie crumbs on the bottom.
2. In a bowl, beat cream cheese, eggs, rum, vanilla and nutmeg. Whisk well and spread over the cookie crumbs.
3. Place in the air fryer and cook at 340F for 20 minutes.
4. Cool and keep in the refrigerator.
5. Slice and serve.

Nutritional Facts Per Serving
- Calories: 412
- Fat: 12g
- Carb: 20g
- Protein: 6g

Strawberry Pie

| Prep time: 10 minutes | Cook time: 20 minutes | Servings: 12 |

Ingredients for the crust
- Coconut – 1 cup, shredded
- Sunflower seeds – 1 cup
- Butter – ¼ cup

For the filling
- Gelatin – 1 tsp.
- Cream cheese – 8 ounces
- Strawberries – 4 ounces
- Water – 2 tbsp.
- Lemon juice – ½ tbsp.
- Stevia – ¼ tsp.
- Heavy cream – ½ cup
- Strawberries – 8 ounces, chopped for serving

Method

1. Mix sunflower seeds, coconut, butter and salt in a food processor. Pulse and press the mixture on the bottom of a cake pan.
2. Heat up a pan with water over medium heat. Add gelatin and stir until it dissolves. Set aside to cool down.
3. Place the gelatin mixture, 4 ounces strawberries, lemon juice, cream cheese and stevia in a food processor. Blend well.

4. Add heavy cream, stir well and spread over crust. Top with 8 ounces strawberries.
5. Place in the air fryer and cook at 330F for 15 minutes.
6. Keep in the fridge until you serve it.

Nutritional Facts Per Serving
- Calories: 234
- Fat: 23g
- Carb: 6g
- Protein: 7g

Coffee Cheesecake

Prep time: 10 minutes	Cook time: 20 minutes	Servings: 6

Ingredients for the cheesecakes
- Butter – 2 tbsp.
- Cream cheese – 8 ounces
- Coffee – 3 tbsp.
- Eggs – 3
- Sugar – 1/3 cup
- Caramel syrup – 1 tbsp.

For the frosting
- Caramel syrup – 3 tbsp.
- Butter – 3 tbsp.
- Mascarpone cheese – 8 ounces, soft
- Sugar – 2 tbsp.

Method
1. In the blender, mix eggs, cream cheese, 1/3 cup sugar, 1 tbsp. caramel syrup, coffee and 2 tbsp. butter. Pulse very well and spoon into a cupcake pan.
2. Cook in the air fryer at 320F for 20 minutes.
3. Cool and keep in the freezer for 3 hours.
4. Meanwhile, in a bowl, mix mascarpone, 2 tbsp. sugar, 3 tbsp. caramel syrup and 3 tbsp. butter. Blend well and spoon over cheesecakes then serve.

Nutritional Facts Per Serving
- Calories: 254
- Fat: 23g
- Carb: 21g
- Protein: 5g

Special Brownies

Prep time: 10 minutes	Cook time: 17 minutes	Servings: 4

Ingredients
- Egg – 1
- Cocoa powder – 1/3 cup
- Sugar – 1/3 cup
- Butter – 7 tbsp.
- Vanilla extract – ½ tsp.
- White flour – ¼ cup

- Walnuts – ¼ cup, chopped
- Baking powder – ½ tsp.
- Peanut butter – 1 tbsp.

Method

1. Add 6 tbsp. butter and sugar in a pan and heat over medium heat. Stir and cook for 5 minutes. Transfer to a bowl.
2. Add flour, walnuts, baking powder, egg, cocoa powder, vanilla extract and salt. Mix well and pour into a pan.
3. In a bowl, mix peanut butter and 1 tbsp. butter. Heat up in the microwave for a few seconds. Mix well and drizzle over the brownie mixture.
4. Place the pan in the air fryer and bake at 320F for 17 minutes.
5. Cool, cut and serve.

Nutritional Facts Per Serving

- Calories: 223
- Fat: 32g
- Carb: 3g
- Protein: 6g

Conclusion

Fried food is delicious, and most of us love it. However, the problem is that it is not good for our bodies. The air fryer is a tremendously popular machine that cooks food in one of the healthiest and tastiest ways imaginable. The air fryer helps you cook food without using much oil. As a result, you consume less calories, stay healthy and avoid weight gain. This complete air fryer cookbook will take care of your limited cooking time and provide you with delicious recipes.

Thank you

Before you go, I just wanted to say thank you for purchasing my book.

You could have picked from dozens of other books on the same topic but you took a chance and chose this one.

So, a HUGE thanks to you for getting this book and for reading all the way to the end.

Now I wanted to ask you for a small favor. **Could you please consider posting a review on the platform? Reviews are one of the easiest ways to support the work of authors.**

This feedback will help me continue to write the type of books that will help you get the results you want. So if you enjoyed it, please let me know.

www.ingramcontent.com/pod-product-compliance
Lightning Source LLC
Chambersburg PA
CBHW052056110526
44591CB00013B/2231